GENESIS THROUGH JOSHUA
Teacher's Manual

by Emily Fischer

Designed by
Ned Bustard

D1261800

veritas
PRESS

First Edition 2001

Copyright ©2001 Veritas Press
www.VeritasPress.com
800-922-5082

ISBN 978-1-930710-90-0

All rights reserved. Permission is granted to make unlimited photocopies of this entire manual for the school or homeschool that purchased this manual. Otherwise, no part of this book may be reproduced without permission from Veritas Press, except by a reviewer who may quote brief passages in a review; nor may any part of this book be reproduced, stored in a retrieval system or transmitted in any form by any means, electronic, mechanical, photocopying, recording or otherwise, without prior permission from Veritas Press.

Printed in the United States of America.

GENESIS THROUGH JOSHUA
How to use this Manual

We hope this guide will be helpful as you study Genesis through Joshua this year. You are about to take a journey through the past where you can see God's providence on a daily basis. Imagine being Noah as he labored over his ark for years, or Moses as he led God's people out of bondage. The Israelites were able to see God crush an entire civilization as He destroyed the Egyptians with plagues. God was faithful to His people through the years just as He is today. What a joy it is for young children to come to realize God's faithfulness as they learn from the past.

The Veritas Press Bible Curriculum was designed to be used as a tool for understanding the Scriptures and cannot be used apart from the Bible. The cards are meant to give students a smaller body of information that they can more easily assimilate. The answers to questions on the worksheets and tests can all be found on the cards, but we strongly recommend that each account is read in the Bible sometime during the week. The *Bible Reading* project is the first project for each card to encourage time spent directly in the Bible. This project reinforces the information on the card and also asks about details and facts that are not listed on the card. Teachers should encourage students to look for new information as they read from the Bible.

There are 32 events/people featured in the cards in this series. That is approximately one per week. A few of the cards have extra projects which may spread into the following week. The projects are only suggestions, so use your imagination and have fun with your group. You will note that the projects vary to appeal to different ages. You may choose the ones you think are appropriate for your group. If you are using this series for second grade or below, you may need to read some of it orally for the first six weeks; after that three times a week is usually enough. You will also want to sing the song daily for the first few weeks until it is memorized. Remember, the reason for the song is to help memorize the chronology of the events. It is also good to have the children recite events in proper order, rather than singing it after the song has been memorized. A sample school week might be planned as follows:

MONDAY: Sing the song (you may want to have a student come to the front of the room and hold up a flashcard as the class sings.) Present the new card. Read what it says on the back and discuss it. Allow different students to read it out loud if you can. Then allow the students to answer questions on the worksheet. The questions are based on information on the cards. If you are working with second grade or below, they may be asked to do this orally for the first part of the year.

TUESDAY: Sing the song. Return the graded worksheet and go over it allowing students to correct their answers. Read the account in the Bible and then complete the Bible Reading project.

WEDNESDAY: Sing the song. Orally review questions from the worksheet. Do one of the projects.

THURSDAY: Sing the song. Orally review questions from this card's worksheet and from previous events. Obviously you cannot review every question every day, so do a sampling. Assign different children different sources from the resource list on the card and allow them to look up the information and share it with the class.

FRIDAY: Give test. Use remaining time for class instruction and drill.

Having fun makes it easy to learn. Using the cards for games is one way. Ask the children to shuffle them and then see who can get their cards in order the fastest. Or have four to six students mix up their cards and then play Go Fish. This allows them to get familiar with the titles. Or you can go to a large room and see who can make their own timeline the fastest. A good way to drill questions in a classroom is to divide the children into two teams and ask questions in order. Teams receive a point for each right answer.

We have found one of the best ways to file and protect the cards is to laminate them, punch a hole in the top right corner, and keep them on a large ring. The children can add the newest card and also have the previous cards handy. Another idea is to laminate them, put Velcro strips on the card and on the wall, and start a timeline that children can put up and take down over and over again. An extra set of cards mounted at the end of the room for a reference timeline is a good idea too.

Each worksheet, test, or writing assignment should receive three grades: one each for Content, Grammar and Linguistics (Spelling).

CONTENT: On a scale of 1 to 15, a grade is given for completeness of the answer to a question. This grade is applied to their Bible grade. If your grading scale is different from 1 to 15, use yours.

GRAMMAR: The child should answer the questions in a complete sentence in which they first restate the question. For example: *What is the Scripture reference for Creation? The Scripture reference for Creation is Genesis 1–2.* Initially in second grade the teacher may want to write a portion of the sentence on the board for the students to copy until they learn to do this correctly on their own. For example: *The Scripture reference for Creation is _____ .* The students would then fill in the rest. As the weeks go by gradually wean them until they are able to do this on their own. Second graders adjust to this in about six weeks. Sentences should begin with a capital letter and end with an appropriate punctuation mark. As the year progresses you can grade more strictly for grammar. This grade should be applied to an application grade in grammar, but should not affect Bible content grades. We suggest application at twenty percent of the overall grade.

LINGUISTICS: The children should spell all words correctly. You should deduct for misspelled words once the rule for spelling a particular word has been mastered. For example: *I before e except after c.* Once this has been covered, a child's grade would be reduced if they spelled *priest as preist.* If they are using a Bible card to do their worksheet they should be taught that those words should be spelled correctly. This grade would be applied towards a linguistics application grade. Again we suggest twenty percent, but not to affect their Bible grade.

When you look at the tests you will see that there are not the same number of questions on each test or worksheet. We assign five points per question, with the listings of the chronology receiving two points per item listed. Partial credit may be counted because the questions are essay, and they may have portions correct.

Some students may ask why they are receiving three grades on each paper. We believe that it is important for a student to realize that grammar and linguistics matter in Bible class as well as in grammar class. All three contribute to help make students understood by others, and are thus intertwined.

CHURCHES: We have provided pages in the back of the manual for using with this program in a Sunday school setting. These pages should be photocopied for each student and folded horizontally to create small booklets. There is more material in these booklets than can be completed during an average Sunday school time period. This calls for flexibility and creativity on the part of the Teacher. Some may even want to spread the study of a card over several weeks to cover the event in sufficient detail. Projects in the body of this manual can be used to supplement or even replace what is contained in the booklets depending on the needs of the class. Teachers should encourage parents to have their children complete the booklets, listen to the Bible song and use the flashcards to review the information during the week to reinforce learning.

Finally we welcome your feedback and comments. We hope that his resource will enrich the education of those children entrusted to you, and will help them understand the comprehensive responsibility that God requires of them.

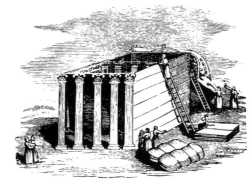

ERECTION OF TABERNACLE.

GENESIS THROUGH JOSHUA
Table of Contents

CREATION
Worksheet

1. What is the Scripture reference for this card?

   _____

   _____

2. Was there ever a time when God did not exist?

   _____

   _____

3. Who created the world and all that is in it?

   _____

   _____

4. In how many days was the world created?

   _____

   _____

5. List what was created or done on each day.

   _____

   _____

   _____

   _____

   _____

   _____

   _____

   _____

   _____

CREATION
Project 1—Bible Reading

Read this story in Genesis 1. Unscramble the words below on the left and then draw a line to connect the words with the phrases on the right that go with them.

Gen. 1:2   *kandesrs*   God told the creatures to
                               _____ and fill the earth.

Gen. 1:3   *blgit*   God saw that everything
                               was _____.

Gen. 1:22   *ultylimp*   _____ was on the
                               face of the deep.

Gen. 1:26   *gamei*   God made man in
                               his own _____.

Gen. 1:28   *oniondim*   God said, "Let there
                               be _____."

Gen. 1:6   *mimatrenf*   God told man to have
                               _____ over the earth.

Gen. 1:31   *odog*   The _____ divided the waters
                               above from the waters below.

CREATION
Project 2—Making Your Own World

Help students remember the days of creation by physically "creating" a world in a large tub. Each day you will add something to your mini-world to show what God created that day. Involve the students by having them bring in objects to put in the world. You may want to combine some of the days over the course of the week in order to go through the days of creation in a typical school week.

Day 1:
Place a big lamp over a tub of water to show how God made light on the first day.

Day 2:
Remove half of the water to show the distinction between the heavens above and the waters below.

Day 3:
Put some of the water from the tub into a shallow plastic container. Remove all extra water and put dirt around your "mini-lake" to show the separation of seas and land. Have samples of small rocks, moss, twigs, and other vegetation so the students can landscape the earth.

Day 4:
Add the sun, moon, and stars. Students may affix pictures/ stickers to the sides of the tub or dangle objects over the top of the tub.

Day 5:
Add creatures of the sky and sea. Plan ahead and encourage students to bring in small plastic figures of these creatures.

Day 6:
Add more plastic figures of animals that dwell on land. Also add figures of Adam and Eve.

CREATION
Project 3—Mural

Make a mural depicting what was created on each day. Divide a large sheet of paper into six sections. Label each section Day 1, Day 2, Day 3, etc. Have students search magazines for pictures or cut out parts of pictures of things that God created. Glue the pictures in the appropriate section of the mural. Students may make individual murals or work together to make a giant class mural.

CREATION
Test

1. What is the Scripture reference for this card?

   _____

   _____

2. Who created the world and all that is in it?

   _____

   _____

   _____

3. List what was created or done on each day.

   Day 1:   Day 5:

   _____   _____

   _____   _____

   _____

   Day 2:   Day 6:

   _____   _____

   _____   _____

   _____

   Day 3:   Day 7:

   _____   _____

   _____   _____

   _____

   Day 4:

   _____

   _____

   _____

THE FALL IN THE GARDEN
Worksheet

1. What is the Scripture reference for this card?

   _____

   _____

2. How did the devil disguise himself when he came to Eve?

   _____

   _____

3. What did the devil tempt Eve to do?

   _____

   _____

4. What did Adam do when Eve gave the fruit to him?

   _____

   _____

5. What had God told Adam about the fruit of the Tree
   of Knowledge?

   _____

   _____

6. What did God curse because of Adam and Eve's sin?

   _____

   _____

7. How had man's relationship with God changed?

   _____

   _____

   _____

THE FALL IN THE GARDEN
Project 1—Bible Reading

Read Genesis 3 to find the answers to the following:

1. The deceiver was the _____.

2. Eve and Adam ate _____.

3. They sewed _____ into coverings.

4. After Adam and Eve sinned they _____ from God.

5. The serpent was cursed to crawl on his _____.

6. Eve would have great _____ in bearing children.

7. Adam would have to _____ for food and the ground would bring forth
   _____ and _____.

8. God made Adam and Eve _____ to wear.

9. God drove them out of the Garden and placed _____ to guard it.

THE FALL IN THE GARDEN
Project 2—Cherubim

The ancient historian Josephus said no one in his day could even conjecture the shape of the cherubim found in the liturgical art found in Solomon's temple. Ezekiel describes them as having four faces and four wings. In Revelation they are covered with eyes and have six wings and combined the likeness of a lion, ox, eagle and a man. Monstrous sculptures of this sort were fashioned in Egypt and Assyria (the example of cherubim on the right was found at the Palace of Konyunjik). In the New Testament, the messengers of God appear as young men, bright as lightning.

Make a clay model of a cherubim like the ones God put in the Garden of Eden to guard the Tree of Life. Refer to Genesis 3:24 to find what weapon the cherubim had for this job.

THE FALL IN THE GARDEN
Project 3

Have students draw scenes depicting the Fall.
Students may cut out and use the quotes
or write their own quotes. Before allow-
ing the students to cut out the quotes
and draw the scenes, go through
each quote and
have students
identify
who said
each quote.

THE SERPENT DECEIVED ME, AND I ATE.

HAS GOD INDEED SAID, "YOU SHALL NOT EAT OF EVERY TREE OF THE GARDEN"?

THE WOMAN WHOM YOU GAVE TO BE WITH ME, SHE GAVE ME OF THE TREE, AND I ATE.

WHAT IS THIS YOU HAVE DONE?

YOU WILL NOT SURELY DIE. FOR GOD KNOWS THAT IN THE DAY YOU EAT OF IT YOUR EYES WILL BE OPENED, AND YOU WILL BE LIKE GOD, KNOWING GOOD AND EVIL.

WHERE ARE YOU?

WHO TOLD YOU THAT YOU WERE NAKED? HAVE YOU EATEN FROM THE TREE OF WHICH I COMMANDED YOU THAT YOU SHOULD NOT EAT?

I HEARD YOUR VOICE IN THE GARDEN, AND I WAS AFRAID BECAUSE I WAS NAKED; AND I HID MYSELF.

WE MAY EAT THE FRUIT OF THE TREES OF THE GARDEN BUT OF THE FRUIT OF THE TREE WHICH IS IN THE MIDST OF THE GARDEN, GOD HAS SAID "YOU SHALL NOT EAT IT, NOR SHALL YOU TOUCH IT, LEST YOU DIE."

THE FALL IN THE GARDEN
Test

1. What is the Scripture reference for this card?

   _____

   _____

2. Who disguised himself and came to Eve?

   _____

   _____

3. What was Eve tempted to do?

   _____

   _____

   _____

4. What did Adam do with the fruit?

   _____

   _____

   _____

5. What had God forbidden Adam and Eve to do?

   _____

   _____

   _____

6. What happened to the ground because of Adam and Eve's sin?

   _____

   _____

7. How had man's relationship with God changed?

   _____

   _____

   _____

CAIN AND ABEL
Worksheet

1. What is the Scripture reference for this card?

   _____

   _____

2. Who was the first child of Adam and Eve?

   _____

   _____

3. What job did Cain do?

   _____

   _____

4. What job did Abel do?

   _____

   _____

5. What offering did Cain bring to God?

   _____

   _____

6. What offering did Abel bring to God?

   _____

   _____

7. With whose offering was God pleased?

   _____

   _____

8. Which son murdered his brother?

   _____

   _____

CAIN AND ABEL
Project 1—Bible Reading

Read Genesis 4. Using your Bible find who said each quote below. Write their names in the blanks. The quotes are listed in the order in which they occurred in the story.

1. "I have acquired a man from the Lord." _____

2. "Why are you angry, and why has your countenance fallen?" _____

3. "Where is Abel your brother?" _____

4. "Am I my brother's keeper?" _____

5. "I shall be a fugitive and a vagabond on the earth, and it will happen that anyone who finds me will kill me." _____

6. "Therefore, whoever kills Cain, vengeance shall be taken on him sevenfold."

   _____

CAIN AND ABEL
Project 2

What do these pictures have to do with the story of Cain and Abel? In the blanks below the pictures write an explanation of how each picture represents part of the story of Cain and Abel. Hint: The pictures are in the order in which they relate to the story.

_____   _____
_____   _____
_____   _____
_____   _____

_____   _____
_____   _____
_____   _____
_____   _____

CAIN AND ABEL
Project 3

Make fancy letters to spell out the names of CAIN and/or ABEL. Each letter should include something that has to do with the person. The name should be written vertically and next to each letter write a sentence explaining how its design relates to the person. Below is an example of how you might write Eve's name.

 *Eve lived with Adam in the Garden of Eden.*

 *The serpent tempted Eve.*

 Eve ate the fruit of the Tree of Knowledge.

Here are some ideas to get started. With which person would each item go?
(Some may fit both but the explanation would be different.)

wheat

rock

sheep

blood

olives

altar

CAIN AND ABEL
Test

1. What is the Scripture reference for this card?

   _____

   _____

2. Who were the parents of Cain and Abel?

   _____

   _____

3. What job did Cain do?

   _____

   _____

4. What offering did Abel bring to God?

   _____

   _____

5. With whose offering was God pleased?

   _____

   _____

   _____

6. _____ murdered _____.

7. What happened to the murderer?

   _____

   _____

   _____

   _____

CAIN AND ABEL
Test

8. List all of the titles, Scripture references, and dates studied so far.

_____

_____

_____

ENOCH AND METHUSELAH
Worksheet

1. What is the Scripture reference for this card?

   _____

   _____

2. Who was the godly child that Adam and Eve had after Cain murdered Abel?

   _____

   _____

3. Enoch's life was characterized by consistent _____

   and _____ .

4. What did the Lord do for Enoch since he was so pleased with Enoch?

   _____

   _____

   _____

5. Enoch is the _____ generation after Adam in _____

   godly line.

6. What does the number seven represent in the Scriptures?

   _____

   _____

   _____

7. How is Methuselah related to Enoch?

   _____

   _____

   _____

ENOCH AND METHUSELAH
Worksheet, Page 2

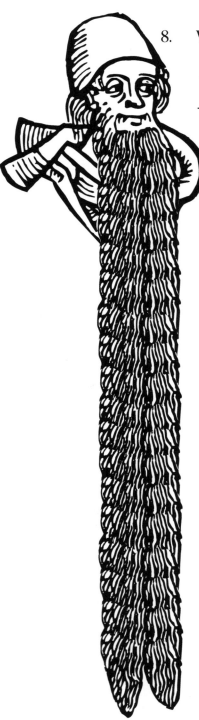

8. What was special about Methuselah?

_____

_____

_____

9. How is Methuselah related to Noah?

_____

_____

_____

Enoch and Methuselah
Project 1—Bible Reading

Read Gen. 5:21-32 and fill in the timeline. Can you calculate how many years are between Enoch and Methuselah's deaths?

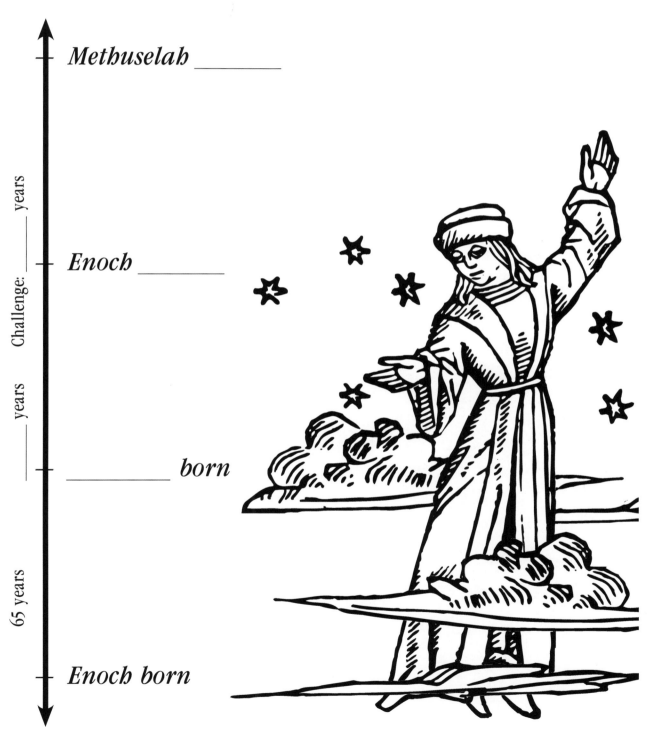

Methuselah _____

_____ years Challenge: _____ years

Enoch _____

_____ years

_____ born

65 years

Enoch born

ENOCH AND METHUSELAH
Project 2—Chart

People lived a lot longer in the days before Noah. Methuselah lived the longest of all people that the Bible records. Fill in the chart with the ages of Adam and his godly line. Use the Bible references to look up each man's age. Each verse is located in Genesis 5.

Ages of Adam's Godly Line to Methuselah

NAME	AGE
Adam (v5)	
Seth (v8)	
Enosh (v11)	
Kenan (v14)	
Mahalel (v17)	
Jared (v20)	
Enoch (v23)	
Methuselah (v27)	

Now put the men in order by how long they lived. Start with the man who lived the longest.

_____

_____

_____

_____

_____

_____

_____

_____

ENOCH AND METHUSELAH
Test

1. What is the Scripture reference for this card?

    _____

    _____

2. Who was the godly child that Adam and Eve had after Cain murdered Abel?

    _____

    _____

    _____

3. Describe Enoch.

    _____

    _____

    _____

4. What was unique about Enoch?

    _____

    _____

    _____

5. What does the number seven represent in the Scriptures?

    _____

    _____

    _____

6. What was special about Methuselah?

    _____

    _____

    _____

7. Methuselah was Enoch's _____.

8. Methuselah was Noah's _____.

ENOCH AND METHUSELAH
Test, Page 2

Review

1. List what was created on each day:

   Day 1 _____

   Day 2 _____

   Day 3 _____

   Day 4 _____

   Day 5 _____

   Day 6 _____

2. What did God tell Adam and Eve would happen if they ate of the Tree of Knowledge?

   _____

   _____

   _____

3. Who tempted Eve to eat of the Tree of Knowledge?

   _____

   _____

4. What job did Abel do?

   _____

   _____

   _____

5. List all of the titles and Scripture references studied so far.

   _____

   _____

   _____

   _____

THE FLOOD
Worksheet

1. What is the Scripture reference for this card?

   _____

   _____

2. What did God observe about man?

   _____

   _____

3. Who found grace in the eyes of the Lord?

   _____

   _____

4. What was to be put in the ark?

   _____

   _____

   _____

5. How long did it rain?

   _____

   _____

   _____

6. What happened to all of the people except Noah and his family?

   _____

   _____

THE FLOOD
Worksheet, Page 2

7. What did God promise Noah after the flood?

_____

_____

_____

_____

_____

8. What sign of the covenant did God give?

_____

_____

_____

THE FLOOD
Project 1—Bible Reading

Read the account of the Flood in Genesis. Then fill in the text and crossword puzzle below.

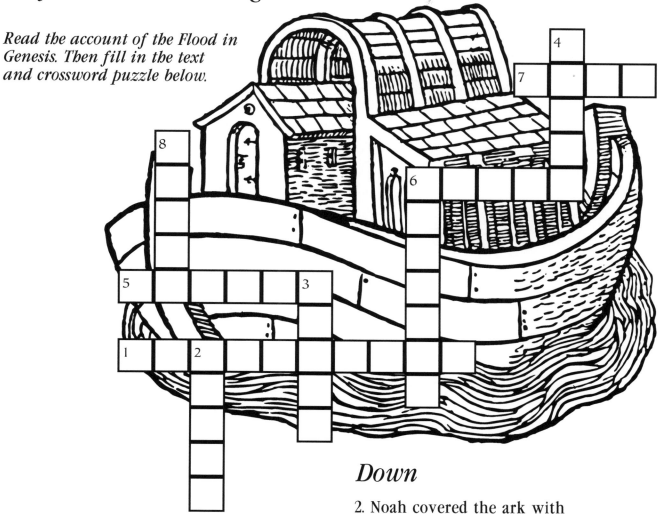

Down

2. Noah covered the ark with

_____ .

3. The ark had _____ decks.

4. Noah took _____ of each of

the clean animals.

6. God made the_____ a sign

that he would never again destroy the

earth with a flood.

8. The first thing Noah built when he left

the ark was an _____ .

Across

1. God told Noah to build an ark out of

_____ .

5. The ark settled after the flood on the

mountains of _____ .

6. Noah first sent a _____ out

of the ark.

7. The second dove came back with an

olive _____ in her mouth.

THE FLOOD
Project 2—An Interview with the Animals

Pretend you are interviewing animals that came off the ark.
Write an answer for each animal including details from the story.

Reporter: Mr. Monkey, how did you get inside that big boat?

MONKEY:

_____

_____

_____

Reporter: Why did you have to go in the ark, Mrs. Squirrel?

SQUIRREL:

_____

_____

_____

Reporter: Mr. Skunk, some animals don't like your smell.

    Why weren't you lonely on the ark?

SKUNK:

_____

_____

_____

Reporter: Miss Ant, there were lots of animals on the ark.

    Were there any humans? If there were humans on the ark, who were they?

ANT:

_____

_____

_____

_____

THE FLOOD
Project 2—An Interview with the Animals, Page 2

Reporter: You probably got tired of being careful not to step on other animals, Mr. Elephant. You must have wanted to get out of the ark. What was going on outside the ark that made it better to be inside rather than outside?

ELEPHANT:

_____

_____

_____

_____

_____

Reporter: Mrs. Snake, how long did you have to slither around in the ark?

SNAKE:

_____

_____

_____

Reporter: You must have become seasick, Mr. Bear. But then all of a sudden, the tossing and turning stopped. What had happened to the ark?

BEAR:

_____

_____

_____

Reporter: Mr. Raven, you had a pretty important job. What did you do?

RAVEN:

_____

_____

_____

THE FLOOD
Project 2—An Interview with the Animals, Page 3

Reporter: What was it like when you left the ark the first time, Mrs. Dove?

DOVE:

_____

_____

Reporter: When you came back from your second trip out of the ark, why was everyone so excited, Mrs. Dove?

DOVE:

_____

_____

_____

Reporter: Mr. Dove, your wife went on a third trip out of the ark. What did Noah tell you probably happened to her?

DOVE:

_____

_____

_____

_____

Reporter: Mr. Pig, you were quite fortunate to not be sacrificed like each of the clean animals when Noah got off the ark. What did you see in the sky to promise that the earth would never be flooded again?

PIG:

_____

_____

_____

_____

THE FLOOD
Test

1. What is the Scripture reference for this card?

_____

_____

2. God observed that man was _____, and so he said he would _____ man.

3. What was special about Noah?

_____

_____

4. What did God command Noah to do?

_____

_____

5. What was Noah to do with a male and female of every species?

_____

_____

_____

6. What happened for forty days and nights?

_____

_____

7. What did God promise Noah after the flood?

_____

_____

_____

8. What sign of the covenant did God give?

_____

_____

_____

THE FLOOD
Test, Page 2

Review

1. How was Adam punished because of his sin in the Garden of Eden?

   _____

   _____

2. Who is the "seed" of the woman that God promised would come and crush Satan?

   _____

   _____

3. What offering did Cain bring to God?

   _____

   _____

   _____

4. Fill in the blanks with either *Cain* or *Abel*.

   _____ murdered _____ .

5. What was special about Methuselah?

   _____

   _____

6. List all of the titles and Scripture references studied so far.

   _____

   _____

   _____

   _____

   _____

God's Covenant with Noah
Worksheet

1. What is the Scripture reference for this card?

   _____

   _____

2. A _____ is like a promise.

3. Who participated in the first covenant that is described in the Bible?

   _____

   _____

   _____

4. What did God promise to Noah and his descendants?

   _____

   _____

   _____

   _____

5. What was the sign that God gave Noah to confirm his covenant?

   _____

   _____

   _____

   _____

GOD'S COVENANT WITH NOAH
Worksheet, Page 2

6. What did Noah remember every time he saw the sign of the covenant?

_____

_____

_____

_____

GOD'S COVENANT WITH NOAH
Project 1—Bible Reading

Read Gen. 1:29 and 9:1-17. In the basket on the left draw examples of what Noah was allowed to eat before the Flood (see Gen. 1:29) and on the right draw examples of what we are allowed to eat now. Then color the picture, adding the missing sign of God's covenant.

GOD'S COVENANT WITH NOAH
Project 2

The first covenant that the Bible talks about is the covenant between _____

and _____. God promised _____.

A covenant is an agreement between two people. God gave Noah a sign to confirm the cov-

enant. The sign of God's covenant was a _____.

The colors of the rainbow are red, orange, yellow, green, blue, indigo, and violet. An easy way to remember the order of the colors is by the first letters of each color: ROYGBIV. (Think of these letters like a man's name: Roy G. Biv) Use the letters ROYGBIV to write words or phrases that have to do with the story of Noah's Ark and God's Covenant with Noah. Begin each word or phrase with a letter for the colors of the rainbow. Students may then color the bands of the rainbow with the appropriate colors.

R
O
Y
G
B
I
V

GOD'S COVENANT WITH NOAH
Test

1. What is the Scripture reference for this card?

   _____

   _____

2. Describe a covenant.

   _____

   _____

   _____

   _____

3. _____ and _____ participated in the first covenant that

   is described in the Bible.

4. What did God promise to Noah?

   _____

   _____

   _____

   _____

5. The promise was for Noah and his _____.

6. What was the sign that God gave Noah to confirm his covenant?

   _____

   _____

   _____

7. What should you remember every time you see the sign of God's covenant with Noah?

   _____

   _____

   _____

GOD'S COVENANT WITH NOAH
Test, Page 2

Review

1. Was there ever a time when God did not exist?

   _____

   _____

2. What did Satan tell Eve would happen if she ate of the Tree of Knowledge?

   _____

   _____

   _____

3. Who were the parents of Cain and Abel?

   _____

   _____

4. With whose offering (Cain or Abel) was God pleased?

   _____

   _____

5. What was special about Enoch?

   _____

   _____

6. List all of the titles and Scripture references studied so far.

   _____

   _____

   _____

   _____

   _____

THE TOWER OF BABEL
Worksheet

1. What is the Scripture reference for this card?

   _____

   _____

2. How many languages were spoken on earth before the Tower of Babel was built?

   _____

   _____

   _____

3. Of what did the people become proud?

   _____

   _____

   _____

4. How did God curse the people because of their pride?

   _____

   _____

   _____

5. What is the tower that some people believe may be the Tower of Babel?

   _____

   _____

   _____

TOWER OF BABEL
Project 1—Bible Reading

Read Genesis 11 and complete these statements.

1. The whole earth spoke one _____.

2. They made _____ of stone and _____ for mortar.

3. They set out to build a _____ and a _____ whose top was in the _____.

4. The Lord came down and _____ their language and _____ them all over the face of the earth.

5. This place is called _____.

TOWER OF BABEL
Project 2

Use the code below to translate the statements in the boxes. Then cut out each statement along the lines and arrange them in the order in which they occurred in the story. Glue the statements to the sections of the tower on the next page putting the first to occur at the top of the tower and the next to occur directly under it and so forth. In the base of the tower make up your own code. Using your code write a coded statement about any previous Bible card studied in each of the bottom two blocks on the tower. Have a partner translate your coded statements.

A B C D E F G H I J K L M N

O P Q R S T U V W X Y Z

TOWER OF BABEL
Project 3—Biblical Art Study

Pieter Bruegel (about 1525-69) was usually known as Pieter Bruegel the Elder (to distinguish him from his elder son) or "Peasant Bruegel" due to his subjects: peasant life, proverbs and genre scenes, and New Testament topics set among common folks of contemporary Flanders. He spelled his name Brueghel until 1559, when for some unknown reason he changed it. His sons retained the "h" in the spelling of their names. Pieter Bruegel the Elder, generally considered the greatest Flemish painter of the 16th century, was probably born in Breda in the Duchy of Brabant. Accepted as a master in the Antwerp painters' guild in 1551, he was apprenticed to Coecke van Aelst, a leading Antwerp artist, sculptor, architect, and designer of tapestry and stained glass. Bruegel traveled to Italy in 1551 or 1552, completing a number of paintings, mostly landscapes, and then he returned home in 1553, settling in Antwerp. In 1563 Bruegel married Mayken, the daughter of Pieter Coeck and Mayken Verhulst Bessemers. His mother-in-law was also a painter, engaged in miniatures. Later, after the death of her son-in-law, she would give the first lessons in painting to his famous sons, Pieter and Jan. The couple settled in Brussels.

Bruegel the Elder's paintings are full of zest and fine detail while they expose human weaknesses and follies. Bruegel's art is often seen as the last phase in the development of a long tradition of Netherlandish painting beginning with Jan van Eyck in the 15th century. This tradition transformed the abstraction of medieval art into a more empirical view of reality. Bruegel clearly rejected the influences of Italian Renaissance art and its classical foundations, which dominated the work of many of his Flemish contemporaries. Rather than muscular nudes and idealized scenes, Bruegel's art portrays figures observed from nature acting out realistic situations in believable contemporary settings.

In subject matter he ranged widely, from conventional Biblical scenes and parables of Christ to mythological portrayals; religious allegories in the style of Hieronymus Bosch; and social satires. Bruegel died in Brussels between Sept. 5 and 9, 1569. The surviving pictures of Bruegel are few in number—under fifty. Bruegel's pictures have been variously interpreted as referring to the beliefs of different religious thinkers, to the conflicts between Roman Catholicism and Protestantism, to the political domination of the Lowlands by the Spanish, and as visual equivalents to dramatic allegories performed publicly by Flemish societies of rhetoric.

TOWER OF BABEL
Project 3—Biblical Art Study

Using the artwork on the cover of this manual or the image on this sheet, discuss Bruegel's The Tower of Babel.

1. How is the confusion of Babel shown in the construction of the building?

    _____

    _____

2. What is Nimrod doing in the painting?

    _____

    _____

3. What classic Roman building seems to be the inspiration for Bruegel's nonsensical tower?

    _____

    _____

THE TOWER OF BABEL
Test

1. What is the Scripture reference for this card?

   _____

   _____

2. Before the Tower of Babel, the people of the earth

   spoke _____ language.

3. What did the people try to build to the heavens?

   _____

   _____

   _____

4. Why did God become angry with the people?

   _____

   _____

   _____

5. God cursed them by causing them to speak

   _____

   and to _____ over the face of the earth.

6. What do some people believe about the zigguarat of Marduk?

   _____

   _____

   _____

THE TOWER OF BABEL
Test, Page 2

Review

1. Who ate the fruit of the Tree of Knowledge first?

   _____

   _____

2. What was the offering that Abel brought to God?

   _____

   _____

3. Who was Abel's brother?

   _____

   _____

4. Who was Methuselah's father?

   _____

   _____

5. Who was Methuselah's grandson?

   _____

   _____

6. List all of the titles and Scripture references studied so far.

   _____

   _____

   _____

   _____

   _____

CALL OF ABRAM
Worksheet

1. What is the date for the call of Abram?

   _____

   _____

2. What is the Scripture reference for the call of Abram?

   _____

   _____

3. Where was Abram's home?

   _____

   _____

4. Who was Abram's wife?

   _____

   _____

5. Who went with Abram?

   _____

   _____

   _____

6. Where did Abram settle?

   _____

   _____

   _____

7. What did God tell Abram about the land in which he had settled?

   _____

   _____

   _____

THE CALL OF ABRAM
Project 1—Bible Reading

After reading Genesis 12, 13 you will learn two stories that occurred during Abram's journey. Complete the word find below, but be sure to know what each word has to do with the two events during Abram's journey.

```
C A N N A A N I T E S A D D L D
S E P A R A T E N E D C I V A E
P H A R O A C A N A A N I T E S
A N T S A R A I Q W E L R T Y C
B U L I V E S T O C K S T A R E
D B R S E N D A E N M B V A C N
S L U T E G Y P T N S I S T R D
T E R E B I N T H X T R E E S A
P A B R S E L K J H G S F D T N
H L O T J S A S S F L O C K S T
A Z A S X O S U C U A M N B V S
R S L G J S R S T H N M S S S F
A A E A U T R D S I O D I S S L
O R S L O E E W A S F O A N S U
H A T T C S S L A N D U L Y E K
V H W A K P H A R O A H L I N E
```

Egypt	Sarai	Jordan
Famine	Livestock	Descendants
Pharaoh	Lot	Terebinth trees
Sister	Tents	Altar
Beautiful	Flocks	Land
Plagues	Separate	Canaanites

CALL OF ABRAM
Project 2

Abram showed great faith in obeying God's call. He left so much behind and embraced a lifestyle that was quite different and lacking the comforts to which he was accustomed. On the left side of the page are sentences that describe what Abram's life was like before God called him to leave. To the right of each arrow write a description or draw a picture of Abram's life after he followed God's call.

Abram's life in Ur: After God called Abram:

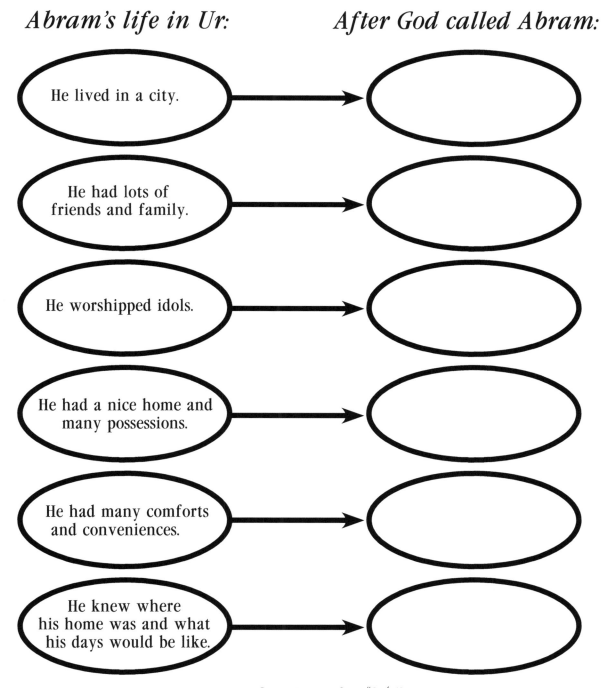

He lived in a city.

He had lots of friends and family.

He worshipped idols.

He had a nice home and many possessions.

He had many comforts and conveniences.

He knew where his home was and what his days would be like.

CALL OF ABRAM
Test

1. What is the date for the call of Abram?

   _____

   _____

2. What is the Scripture reference for the call of Abram?

   _____

   _____

3. Where was Abram's home?

   _____

   _____

4. Who was Sarai?

   _____

   _____

5. Who was Lot?

   _____

   _____

6. Did God tell Abram where he was going before he left?

   _____

   _____

7. Where did Abram settle?

   _____

   _____

   _____

CALL OF ABRAM
Test, Page 2

Review

1. What did God do on the seventh day of creation?

   _____

   _____

2. Who were Cain and Abel's parents?

   _____

   _____

   _____

3. Who found favor in the sight of God and was spared when God decided to destroy man?

   _____

   _____

   _____

4. How did God destroy man?

   _____

   _____

5. What is a covenant?

   _____

   _____

   _____

6. What did God covenant with Noah when he came out of the ark?

   _____

   _____

   _____

CALL OF ABRAM
Review, Page 2

7. List all of the titles and Scripture references studied so far.

_____

_____

_____

_____

_____

_____

_____

_____

GOD'S COVENANT WITH ABRAHAM
Worksheet

1. What is the date for God's covenant with Abraham?

   _____

   _____

2. What is the Scripture reference for God's covenant with Abraham?

   _____

   _____

3. What did God promise Abraham?

   _____

   _____

   _____

4. When God made his covenant with Abraham, Sarah and Abraham were too old to have what?

   _____

   _____

   _____

   _____

5. What animals did Abraham cut in two pieces?

   _____

   _____

   _____

   _____

GOD'S COVENANT WITH ABRAHAM
Worksheet, Page 2

6. In what form did the Lord move between the pieces of the dead animals?

_____

_____

_____

_____

7. What sign did God later give to Abraham?

_____

_____

_____

_____

_____

GOD'S COVENANT WITH ABRAHAM
Project 1—Bible Reading

Read Genesis 15 and use your Bible to fill in the blanks.

THE PROMISE:

1. God promised Abram many _____ that would
   outnumber the _____.

2. God also promised to give Abram _____.

CONFIRMATION OF THE PROMISE:

1. Abram cut a _____, _____,
   and _____ in two pieces and put the pieces along with a pigeon
   and turtledove opposite each other.

2. Abram had to chase away _____.

3. God told Abram that his descendants would serve another nation for _____
   years. Then they would leave that land with great _____
   and return to this _____ which God was promising Abram.

4. A _____ _____ and a _____
   _____ passed between the pieces.

THE SIGN OF THE COVENANT:

1. Gen. 17:10 Every male child was to be _____.

THE NAME CHANGES:

1. Gen. 17:5 Abram's name changed to _____.

2. Gen. 17:15 Sarai's name changed to _____.

GOD'S COVENANT WITH ABRAHAM
Project 2

Explain what each picture has to do with God's covenant with Abraham. Then color the pictures.

1. _____
   _____
   _____
   _____
   _____
   _____

2. _____
   _____
   _____
   _____
   _____
   _____

3. _____
   _____
   _____
   _____
   _____

God's Covenant With Abraham
Test

1. What is the date for God's covenant with Abraham?

    _____

    _____

2. What is the Scripture reference for God's covenant with Abraham?

    _____

    _____

3. What did God promise Abraham?

    _____

    _____

    _____

4. When God made his covenant with Abraham, Sarah and Abraham were too old
    to have _____.

5. What did Abraham do with the heifer, goat, and ram?

    _____

    _____

    _____

6. What did the Lord do in the form of a smoking oven and a burning torch?

    _____

    _____

    _____

7. Did God's promise to Abraham immediately come true?

    _____

    _____

    _____

God's Covenant With Abraham
Test, Page 2

Review

1. In how many days was the world created?

   _____

   _____

2. How was Eve punished for eating the forbidden fruit?

   _____

   _____

3. Who was Adam and Eve's godly child whose descendants include Enoch and Methuselah?

   _____

   _____

4. How was Noah and his family spared from the flood?

   _____

   _____

5. How many languages were spoken on earth before the Tower of Babel was built?

   _____

   _____

6. Who was Sarai?

   _____

   _____

God's Covenant With Abraham
Test, Page 3

Review

7. List all of the titles and Scripture references studied so far.

_____

_____

_____

_____

_____

_____

_____

_____

_____

HAGAR AND ISHMAEL
Worksheet

1. What is the date for Hagar and Ishmael?

   _____

   _____

   _____

2. What is the Scripture reference for Hagar and Ishmael?

   _____

   _____

   _____

3. What had Sarah not been able to give to Abraham?

   _____

   _____

   _____

4. Why did Abraham marry Hagar?

   _____

   _____

   _____

5. How did Sarah treat Hagar when she found out Hagar was going to have a baby?

   _____

   _____

   _____

6. What did the Angel tell Hagar about her descendants?

   _____

   _____

   _____

HAGAR AND ISHMAEL
Worksheet, Page 2

7. What did Abraham do to Hagar when Ishmael scoffed at Isaac's feast?

_____

_____

_____

8. What modern day people are believed to be the descendants of Ishmael?

_____

_____

HAGAR AND ISHMAEL
Project 1—Bible Reading

Read Gen. 16, 21 and then complete the word find below. Be sure to know what each word has to do with the story.

```
W I A S W W S S H A G A R N M M
I S E A I S H M A E L F H O L A
L H L S L T S S R S S L A P K I
D F L E D R D E S P I S E D J D
E M D S E S S S H H S A G W I S
R C C B R K Q R T A S R A A H E
N H E I N I F U X R S A S T G R
S I G F E N S V B S B I R E F V
A L J H S S U O O H O R S R E A
R D K I S P S A E I W A A S D N
A L R N S S R B A C S E S K S T
H E S S L M S I S S H S A I C B
Q S D T A U V W N S O X Y N Z A
P S N M R L K J I G T H G F E E
O P Q R A R C H E R S T U V W D
S N M L I K J I H G F E D C B A
```

childless	fled	weaned
maidservant	spring	waterskin
Hagar	wilderness	bowshot
despised	Ishmael	archer
harsh	Sarai	

Hagar and Ishmael
Project 2

Put the words at the bottom of the page under the woman to which they go in the story.

Sarah	Hagar
_____	_____
_____	_____
_____	_____
_____	_____
_____	_____
_____	_____
_____	_____

maidservant

Isaac

Ishmael

Arabs

ran away

treated the other harshly

Sarai

scoffed at a feast of weaning

90

visited by an angel

HAGAR AND ISHMAEL
Project 3

Rembrandt has sketched out a picture of an angel visiting Hagar in the desert. But it isn't finished! Using a black ink pen, draw over the sketch to make the finished picture, then color it in.

HAGAR AND ISHMAEL
Test

1. What is the date for Hagar and Ishmael?

   _____

   _____

2. What is the Scripture reference for Hagar and Ishmael?

   _____

   _____

3. Whose idea was it for Abraham to take Hagar for his wife?

   _____

   _____

   _____

4. Why did Abraham marry Hagar?

   _____

   _____

   _____

   _____

5. Who was the child born to Hagar and Abraham?

   _____

   _____

   _____

6. What was Hagar told about her descendants?

   _____

   _____

   _____

   _____

Hagar and Ishmael
Test, Page 2

7. What happened to Hagar when Ishmael scoffed at the feast for Isaac?

_____

_____

_____

_____

8. What modern day people are believed to be the descendants of Ishmael?

_____

_____

_____

Review

1. Why did Cain kill Abel?

_____

_____

_____

2. What was Noah to bring into the ark along with his family?

_____

_____

_____

3. What sign did God give that he would not destroy the earth with a flood again?

_____

_____

_____

HAGAR AND ISHMAEL
Test, Page 3

4. What is the tower that some people believe may be the Tower of Babel?

_____

_____

_____

5. How did God curse the people because of their pride in the Tower of Babel?

_____

_____

_____

6. Who was Abram's nephew?

_____

_____

7. List all of the titles and Scripture references studied so far.

_____

_____

_____

_____

_____

_____

_____

_____

_____

_____

SODOM AND GOMORRAH
Worksheet

1. What is the date for Sodom and Gomorrah?

   _____

   _____

2. What is the Scripture reference for Sodom and Gomorrah?

   _____

   _____

3. What did God plan to do to Sodom and Gomorrah?

   _____

   _____

   _____

4. What would God have done if there were ten righteous men living in Sodom and Gomorrah?

   _____

   _____

   _____

5. Who was the only righteous man in those cities?

   _____

   _____

6. What foolish thing did the wife of the righteous man do?

   _____

   _____

   _____

SODOM AND GOMORRAH
Worksheet, Page 2

7. What happened to the wife of the righteous man?

    _____

    _____

    _____

8. What did this event teach Abraham and his descendants?

    _____

    _____

    _____

    _____

SODOM AND GOMORRAH
Project 1—Bible Reading

Read about this story in the Bible *or* The Child's Story Bible, *pages 23, 24.*
Then answer the following questions:

1. Explain how the two angels saved Lot when the wicked people came to his house.

   _____

   _____

   _____

   _____

   _____

2. Where did Lot go after he fled from Sodom and Gomorrah?

   _____

   _____

   _____

   _____

   _____

3. Who was with Lot after he left the cities?

   _____

   _____

   _____

   _____

   _____

   _____

SODOM AND GOMORRAH
Project 2

Diorama Supplies

1' square piece of cardboard (you can also put diorama inside a shoebox)
small boxes (jello, film, medicine size), cardboard tubes
tissue paper: red, orange, and yellow
glue
pipe cleaners
salt
clay
construction paper
scissors
black marker
yarn
felt, fabric

Directions

Paint the small boxes and tubes a sand color. These will be arranged to be buildings of the cities. When the paint is dry use black marker to draw on windows, doors, and other details. Use construction paper to add more details to the cities. Glue the two cities to the cardboard square. Make people by folding 4" pieces of pipe cleaners in half. The crease of the fold is the head. Separate the bottom ends to make legs. Attach another 1" pipe cleaner to make arms. Using paper, fabric and/or felt glue clothes to the pipe cleaner bodies. Use clay and other supplies to make parcels. Yarn can be glued on as hair. Use glue or clay to attach people to the cardboard base. Make a thin pillar out of clay, cover it with glue, and pour salt on it to make Lot's wife.

SODOM AND GOMORRAH
Test

1. What is the date for Sodom and Gomorrah?

   _____

   _____

2. What is the Scripture reference for Sodom and Gomorrah?

   _____

   _____

3. Who pleaded with God to save Sodom and Gomorrah?

   _____

   _____

   _____

4. What needed to be found in Sodom and Gomorrah in order to save the cities?

   _____

   _____

   _____

   _____

5. Who was Lot?

   _____

   _____

   _____

6. What did Lot's wife do during the destruction of Sodom and Gomorrah?

   _____

   _____

   _____

SODOM AND GOMORRAH
Test, Page 2

7. What happened to Lot's wife?

_____

_____

_____

_____

8. What did this event teach Abraham and his descendants?

_____

_____

_____

Review

1. How did the sin of Adam and Eve affect all men?

_____

_____

_____

_____

2. Who was taken into heaven without seeing death?

_____

_____

3. What was Noah told to build?

_____

_____

_____

SODOM AND GOMORRAH
Test, Page 3

4. Why did God cause men to speak many different languages?

   _____

   _____

   _____

5. What did God promise Abraham?

   _____

   _____

   _____

6. Who were Ishmael's father and mother?

   _____

   _____

7. List all of the titles and Scripture references studied so far.

   _____

   _____

   _____

   _____

   _____

   _____

   _____

   _____

   _____

   _____

THE BIRTH AND SACRIFICE OF ISAAC
Worksheet

1. What is the date for the birth and sacrifice of Isaac?

   _____

   _____

2. What is the Scripture reference for the birth and sacrifice of Isaac?

   _____

   _____

3. How old were Abraham and Sarah when they had Isaac?

   _____

   _____

   _____

4. What did God command Abraham to do to Isaac?

   _____

   _____

   _____

5. On what mountain did Abraham build the altar?

   _____

   _____

   _____

6. Who stopped Abraham from sacrificing Isaac?

   _____

   _____

   _____

THE BIRTH AND SACRIFICE OF ISAAC
Worksheet, Page 2

7. What did Abraham really sacrifice on the altar?

_____

_____

8. What about Abraham pleased God?

_____

_____

_____

BIRTH AND SACRIFICE OF ISAAC
Project 1—Bible Reading

Read Genesis 22 and put these events in order from 1–11.

___ Abraham, Isaac, & some men went to the mountains at Moriah.

___ The Angel of the Lord stopped Abraham.

___ Abraham took the ram that was caught in the thicket and sacrificed it.

___ God told Abraham to sacrifice Isaac.

___ Abraham told Isaac that God would provide the offering.

___ Abraham named the place The-Lord-Will-Provide.

___ Abraham built an altar and put wood on it.

___ Abraham told his men that they were going away to worship and would return soon.

___ Isaac was bound to the altar.

___ God promised Abraham again to make his descendants numerous.

___ Abraham took his knife to slay Isaac.

BIRTH AND SACRIFICE OF ISAAC
Project 2–Crossword Puzzle

Across

1. On what mountain did Abraham take his son?
2. What stopped Abraham from sacrificing his son?
3. Whom did God tell Abraham to sacrifice?

Down

4. God provided a _____ to be sacrificed instead of Abraham's son.
5. Where did Abraham find what he actually sacrificed?
6. A sacrifice was placed on an _____.
7. God was pleased with the _____ of Abraham.
8. What did God tell Abraham to do to his son?
9. What about Abraham and Sarah made Isaac's birth mircaulous?

THE BIRTH AND SACRIFICE OF ISAAC
Test

1. What is the date for the birth and sacrifice of Isaac?

    _____

    _____

2. What is the Scripture reference for the birth and sacrifice of Isaac?

    _____

    _____

3. How old were Abraham and Sarah when they had Isaac?

    _____

    _____

4. Why did Abraham take Isaac up onto Mt. Moriah?

    _____

    _____

5. What did Abraham build on Mt. Moriah?

    _____

    _____

6. Who stopped Abraham from harming his son?

    _____

    _____

7. What did Abraham find in the nearby bushes?

    _____

    _____

8. God was pleased with the _____ and _____ of Abraham.

BIRTH AND SACRIFICE OF ISAAC
Test, Page 2

Review

1. Describe how God spared Noah and his family from the flood.

   _____

   _____

   _____

   _____

2. What area of land did God promise to give to Abram and his descendants?

   _____

   _____

   _____

3. God performed a ceremony to confirm his promise to _____ that he would make him a great nation. God had him cut animals in _____ pieces. Then God came down in the form of a _____ and moved between the pieces of the dead animals.

4. Since Sarah was so old and had not had any children, who did Abraham take as a wife so he could have a child?

   _____

   _____

   _____

5. How old was Sarah when she had Isaac?

   _____

   _____

BIRTH AND SACRIFICE OF ISAAC
Test, Page 3

6. List all of the titles and Scripture references studied so far.

_____

_____

_____

_____

_____

_____

_____

_____

_____

_____

_____

_____

ISAAC AND REBEKAH
Worksheet

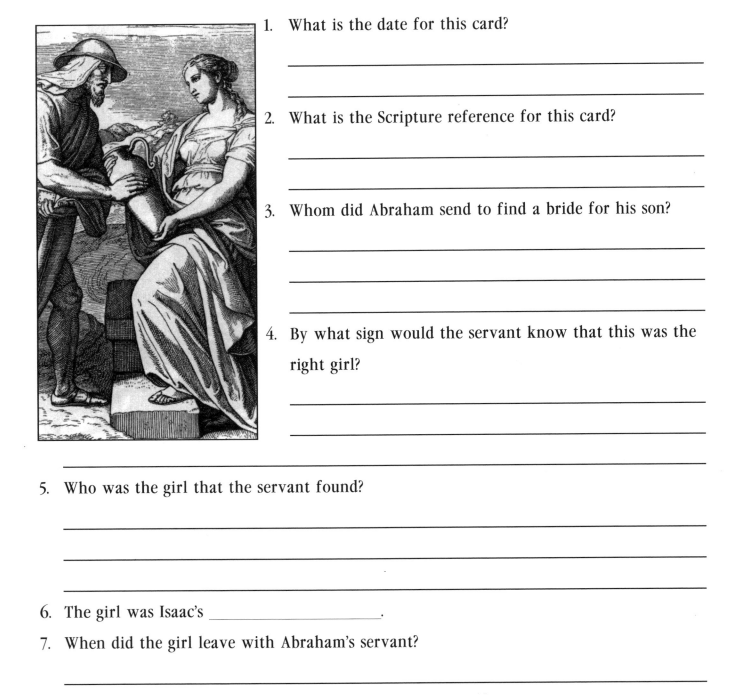

1. What is the date for this card?

   _____

   _____

2. What is the Scripture reference for this card?

   _____

   _____

3. Whom did Abraham send to find a bride for his son?

   _____

   _____

   _____

4. By what sign would the servant know that this was the

   right girl?

   _____

   _____

_____

5. Who was the girl that the servant found?

   _____

   _____

   _____

6. The girl was Isaac's _____.

7. When did the girl leave with Abraham's servant?

   _____

   _____

   _____

ISAAC AND REBEKAH
Project 1—Bible Reading

After reading Genesis 24, complete the following questions:

1. In those days you did not put your hand on the Bible to swear an oath.

   Where did Abraham's servant put his hand to swear the oath? (Gen. 24:9)

   _____

   _____

   _____

2. What did the servant give to Rebekah after she watered his camels? (Gen 24:22)

   _____

   _____

ISAAC AND REBEKAH
Project 1—Bible Reading, Page 2

3. Until when wouldn't the servant eat? (Gen. 24:33)

   _____

   _____

   _____

4. For how many days did Rebekah's brother and mother ask the servant to stay before going back with her? (Gen. 24:55)

   _____

   _____

   _____

5. Who decided that Rebekah would go back with the servant immediately? (Gen. 24:58)

   _____

   _____

   _____

ISAAC AND REBEKAH
Project 2—Jewish Weddings

There are many parts in a traditional wedding that trace back to Bible times. And there are some differences. In the Old Testament, the parents had an influencial role in deciding whom their children would marry. Abraham sent a servant to find a bride for Isaac. Many Christian parents today counsel their children how to chose a good spouse. The Biblical principles of courtship are still helpful to fathers as they seek to protect their daughters and sons in this important decision. Most modern weddings do not include a bride's price or a dowry. In the Old Testament, the bride's price was money paid to the parents of the bride since the parents would be losing the valuable service and labor of their daughter. The dowry was money given to the bride by her father for her to keep. Both the bride's price and the dowry demonstrate that in marriage, a woman was moving from the care and protection of her father to her husband. This idea can still be seen in a modern marriage when the bride's father walks her down the aisle and gives her hand in marriage to the groom.

Today couples have an engagement period which varies in length. In the Bible this time was called a betrothal, and it would usually last about one year. Betrothal was a very serious vow. Even though you were not officially married, you could receive an inheritance from your betrothed's family and you needed a formal divorce to end the betrothal. During both engagements and betrothals, the time is spent in preparing food and special clothes for the actual wedding. The bride wore special clothes including a veil. Grooms during Isaac's days did not wear tuxedos, however. They wore fancy clothes decorated with jewels.

A procession was part of Biblical weddings as well as some modern weddings. In Bible times the groom would walk with his friends to the bride's house. The bride, her bridesmaids and other guests would then walk with the groom and his friends back to his house. You may remember a parable of Jesus that talked about maidens not having enough oil for a wedding procession. The procession was lighted by guests carrying oil lamps. In a modern wedding bridesmaids process up the aisle before the bride, and sometimes small girls will throw flowers in the bride's path as she processes.

The weddings you have attended may look very different from the weddings of Isaac and Rebekah and other couples in Bible times. But the Bible gives all Christians principles to follow in their weddings and all of their married life.

ISAAC AND REBEKAH
Test

1. What is the date for this card?

   _____

   _____

2. What is the Scripture reference for this card?

   _____

   _____

3. What did Abraham send his trusted servant to do?

   _____

   _____

   _____

4. Who was the girl that the servant found?

   _____

   _____

   _____

5. How did the servant know that this was the right girl?

   _____

   _____

   _____

6. How was the girl related to Isaac?

   _____

   _____

   _____

ISAAC AND REBEKAH
Test, Page 2

7. Rebekah left her home the next day with Abraham's servant to

_____

_____

Review

1. List what was created or done on each day.

   Day 1 _____

   Day 2 _____

   Day 3 _____

   Day 4 _____

   Day 5 _____

   Day 6 _____

   Day 7 _____

2. Who was the first child of Adam and Eve?

_____

_____

3. What is a covenant?

_____

_____

_____

4. What were the people of the earth trying to build that would reach the heavens?

_____

_____

_____

ISAAC AND REBEKAH
Test, Page 3

5. Who was Abraham's wife?

   _____

   _____

6. What would God have done if there had been ten righteous men living in
   Sodom and Gomorrah?

   _____

   _____

   _____

7. List all of the titles and Scripture references studied so far.

   _____

   _____

   _____

   _____

   _____

   _____

   _____

   _____

   _____

   _____

   _____

   _____

JACOB AND ESAU
Worksheet

1. What is the date for this card?

   _____

   _____

2. What is the Scripture reference for this card?

   _____

   _____

3. What did God tell Rebekah about the twins she would have?

   _____

   _____

   _____

4. The firstborn son was named _____.

5. The name "Jacob" means _____.

6. What is a birthright?

   _____

   _____

   _____

7. For what did Esau sell his birthright?

   _____

   _____

   _____

8. Isaac was old and _____.

9. Even though Esau had foolishly sold his birthright, what did Isaac still determine to do?

   _____

   _____

   _____

Jacob and Esau
Worksheet, Page 2

10. How did Isaac try to be sure that the son he was blessing was Esau?

_____

_____

_____

_____

11. How did Jacob trick his father?

_____

_____

_____

_____

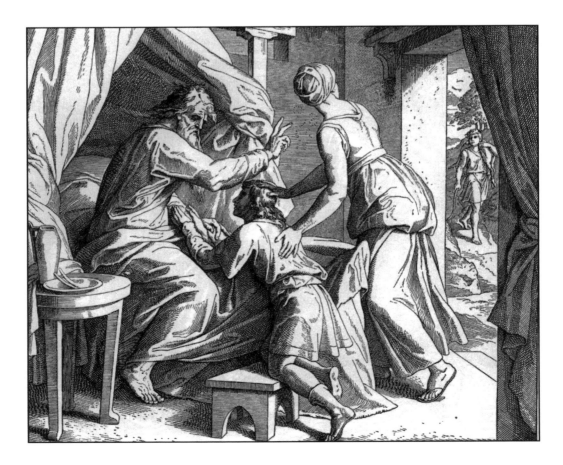

JACOB AND ESAU
Project 1—Bible Reading

1. Read Gen. 25:19-34, 27:1-46. Write a sentence using each of the words below explaining its use in the story.

    heel

    _____

    _____

    lentils

    _____

    _____

    smooth-skinned

    _____

    _____

    blind

    _____

    _____

2. What does Esau plan to do after his father dies?

    _____

    _____

    _____

3. Who overhears Esau's plan?

    _____

    _____

4. To where is Jacob sent?

    _____

    _____

    _____

Jacob and Esau
Project 2—Soup Recipe

Esau sold his birthright for a bowl of soup. Here is a soup recipe that, though good, probably won't make anyone want to give up his birthright.

Middle Eastern Lentil Soup Makes 4 servings

1 cup dried lentils
2 tablespoons olive oil
1 onion, chopped
1 red bell pepper, chopped
1/2 teaspoon ground cumin
1 teaspoon fennel seed
1/4 teaspoon ground red pepper
1/2 teaspoon salt
1 tablespoon lemon juice

1. Rinse lentils, discarding any debris or blemished lentils; drain.
2. Heat oil in large saucepan over medium-high heat until hot. Add onion and bell pepper; cook and stir 5 minutes or until tender. Add cumin, fennel seed and ground red pepper; cook and stir 1 minute.
3. Add 4 cups water and lentils. Bring to a boil. Reduce heat to low. Cover and simmer 20 minutes. Stir in salt. Simmer 5 to 10 minutes more or until lentils are tender. Stir in lemon juice.

For a special touch, top each serving with yellow bell pepper strips.

JACOB AND ESAU
Test

1. What is the date for this card?

   _____

   _____

2. What is the Scripture reference for this card?

   _____

   _____

3. Describe the struggle between Jacob and Esau over the birthright.

   _____

   _____

   _____

   _____

   _____

   _____

   _____

   _____

   _____

   _____

   _____

   _____

   _____

   _____

   _____

Jacob and Esau
Test, Page 2

Review

1. What had God forbidden Adam and Eve to do in the Garden of Eden?

   _____

   _____

   _____

2. What does the number seven represent in the Scriptures?

   _____

   _____

3. What was the sign that God gave to Noah to confirm his promise to never again destroy the earth with a flood?

   _____

   _____

   _____

   _____

4. Tell one thing about God's covenant with Abraham.

   _____

   _____

   _____

   _____

5. How did Sarah treat Hagar when she found out Hagar was going to have a baby?

   _____

   _____

   _____

JACOB AND ESAU
Test, Page 3

6. On what mountain was Abraham told to sacrifice Isaac?

_____

_____

_____

7. List all of the titles and Scripture references studied so far.

_____

_____

_____

_____

_____

_____

_____

_____

_____

_____

_____

_____

_____

_____

_____

JOSEPH AS A SLAVE
Worksheet

1. What is the date for Joseph as a Slave?

   _____

   _____

2. What is the Scripture reference for Joseph as a Slave?

   _____

   _____

3. What did Joseph dream when he was seventeen?

   _____

   _____

   _____

4. Why did Joseph's brothers envy him?

   _____

   _____

   _____

5. What did Joseph's brothers conspire to do?

   _____

   _____

   _____

6. Who convinced his brothers to put Joseph into a pit?

   _____

   _____

   _____

JOSEPH AS A SLAVE
Worksheet, Page 2

7. To whom was Joseph sold?

   _____

   _____

   _____

8. What was done to Joseph's coat so his father would think he was dead?

   _____

   _____

   _____

9. How did Joseph end up in prison?

   _____

   _____

   _____

JOSEPH AS A SLAVE
Project 1—Bible Reading

In Genesis 40 we read of Joseph's days in prison. How did Joseph first become a slave? How did Joseph then become imprisoned? In prison he interpreted the dreams of Pharaoh's chief butler and chief baker. *Draw pictures illustrating what each man saw in his dream. In the space below, write Joseph's interpretation of each dream. Were Joseph's interpretations correct?*

Butler

Baker

JOSEPH AS A SLAVE
Project 2

On two different occasions on this card, Joseph was in bondage. List the following details explaining both situations. Draw pictures of both ways in which Joseph was in bondage.

What kind? _____

_____

Where: _____

_____

How? _____

_____

Why? _____

_____

By whom? _____

_____

What kind? _____

_____

Where? _____

_____

How? _____

_____

Why? _____

_____

By whom? _____

_____

Joseph as a Slave
Test

1. What is the date for Joseph as a Slave?

   _____

   _____

2. What is the Scripture reference for Joseph as a Slave?

   _____

   _____

3. Describe Joseph's dream that made his brothers angry.

   _____

   _____

   _____

   _____

4. What did Joseph's brothers conspire to do?

   _____

   _____

   _____

5. What did Reuben do?

   _____

   _____

   _____

6. How did Joseph become a slave?

   _____

   _____

   _____

   _____

Joseph as a Slave
Test, Page 2

7. In what country was Joseph a slave?

   _____

   _____

   _____

8. Why did Joseph's father think he was dead?

   _____

   _____

   _____

   _____

9. Who falsely accused Joseph so that he was put in prison?

   _____

   _____

   _____

Review

1. Why did God decide to destroy man?

   _____

   _____

2. Where was Abram from originally?

   _____

   _____

Joseph as a Slave
Test, Page 3

3. Tell one thing about Sarah.

_____

_____

_____

4. Who was Hagar's son?

_____

_____

5. Who was the only righteous man living in Sodom and Gomorrah?

_____

6. What did God provide for Abraham to sacrifice instead of his son?

_____

_____

_____

JOSEPH AS A SLAVE
Test, Page 4

7. List all of the titles and Scripture references studied so far.

_____

_____

_____

_____

_____

_____

_____

_____

_____

_____

_____

_____

_____

_____

_____

FAMINE IN EGYPT
Worksheet

1. What is the date for the famine in Egypt?

   _____

   _____

2. What is the Scripture reference for the famine in Egypt?

   _____

   _____

3. Who told Pharaoh of Joseph's ability to interpret dreams?

   _____

   _____

   _____

4. Who did Joseph say gave him the ability to interpret Pharaoh's dreams?

   _____

   _____

   _____

5. What did Pharaoh's dream indicate would happen in the future?

   _____

   _____

   _____

   _____

6. What high position did Pharaoh give Joseph for interpreting his dream?

   _____

   _____

   _____

FAMINE IN EGYPT
Worksheet, Page 2

7. Who came to Egypt to buy grain?

_____

_____

_____

8. What did Pharaoh invite Jacob and his family to do?

_____

_____

_____

_____

FAMINE IN EGYPT
Project 1—Bible Reading

Read Genesis 37 and answer the following questions.

1. In Pharaoh's dream, what did the seven gaunt cows represent?

    _____

    _____

    _____

2. Name the gifts that Pharaoh gave Joseph when he made him second-in-command.

    _____

    _____

    _____

3. What did Joseph at first accuse his brothers of being when they first came to Egypt for his help?

    _____

    _____

    _____

    _____

4. For whom did Joseph send his brothers home to bring back to Egypt?

    _____

    _____

    _____

5. What did Joseph's steward hide in Benjamin's sack?

    _____

    _____

    _____

FAMINE IN EGYPT
Project 2—Family Tree

Pharaoh invited all of Joseph's family to come and live in the land of Joseph. Using your knowledge of the patriarchs, complete the following family tree. See Card 17.

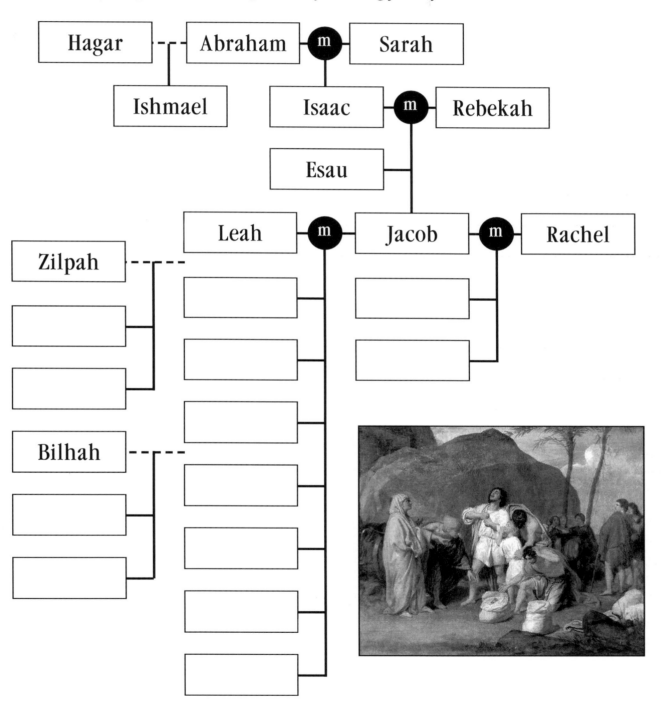

FAMINE IN EGYPT
Project 3—Egyptian Life Booklet

Joseph's family would have seen many different things when they moved to Egypt. Cut out the pages and assemble them as shown. Then study and color these pictures showing Egyptian culture.

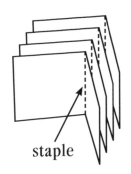

staple

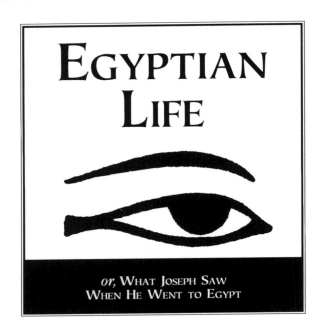

EGYPTIAN LIFE

or, WHAT JOSEPH SAW WHEN HE WENT TO EGYPT

Veritas Press

Animals

Flowers

FAMINE IN EGYPT
Project 3—Egyptian Life Booklet, Page 2

Craftsmen

Food

FAMINE IN EGYPT
Project 3—Egyptian Life Booklet, Page 3

Mummies

Hieroglyphics

Mythology

Pharaohs

FAMINE IN EGYPT
Project 3—Egyptian Life Booklet, Page 4

Papyrus

Cosmetics

Games

Toys

FAMINE IN EGYPT
Test

1. What is the date for the famine in Egypt?

   _____

   _____

2. What is the Scripture reference for the famine in Egypt?

   _____

   _____

3. How did the butler help Pharaoh with the interpretation of his dreams?

   _____

   _____

   _____

4. Pharaoh's dreams indicated that there would be _____ years of _____

   before/after (*circle one*) _____ years of _____.

5. How did Pharaoh reward Joseph for interpreting his dreams?

   _____

   _____

   _____

   _____

6. What did Joseph build to prepare for the famine?

   _____

   _____

   _____

   _____

FAMINE IN EGYPT
Test, Page 2

7. Why did Joseph's brothers come to Egypt?

_____

_____

_____

8. Did Joseph's brothers recognize him at first?

_____

_____

_____

9. Who did Pharaoh invite to come and live in the land of Goshen?

_____

_____

_____

Review

1. Tell two things about God's covenant with Noah.

_____

_____

_____

2. What did God do because of the pride of the people in building the Tower of Babel?

_____

_____

_____

FAMINE IN EGYPT
Test, Page 3

3. What was the sign of the covenant that God made with Abraham?

_____

_____

_____

4. When Hagar ran away because of Sarah's meanness, who found Hagar and promised that God would protect her?

_____

_____

_____

5. How old was Abraham when he had Isaac?

_____

_____

_____

6. How would Abraham's servant know when he had found the right wife for Isaac?

_____

_____

_____

FAMINE IN EGYPT
Test, Page 4

7. List all of the titles and Scripture references studied so far.

_____

_____

_____

_____

_____

_____

_____

_____

_____

_____

_____

_____

_____

_____

_____

TWELVE TRIBES OF ISRAEL
Worksheet

1. What is the date for the twelve tribes of Israel?

   _____

   _____

2. What is the Scripture reference for the twelve tribes of Israel?

   _____

   _____

   _____

3. What had God promised to Abraham?

   _____

   _____

   _____

4. Name the three Patriarchs.

   _____

   _____

5. To what did God change Jacob's name?

   _____

   _____

   _____

6. How many sons did Jacob have?

   _____

   _____

   _____

7. What are the descendents of Jacob's sons known as?

   _____

   _____

THE TWELVE TRIBES OF ISRAEL
Project 1—Bible Reading

In Genesis 49 Jacob gives his final words to his sons. He tells about his sons' past and prophesies about their futures. He also identifies many of them with a symbol or animal. Each tribe has a symbol to represent it. (For a complete illustration of the tribal symbols see the Children's Illustrated Bible, p. 89.) *Draw four of the tribal symbols below and label them with the name of the tribe.*

TWELVE TRIBES OF ISRAEL
Project 2—Twelve Tribes Mobile

On page 89 in *The Children's Illustrated Bible* by Selina Hastings, the symbols for the tribes of Israel are identified. Color the symbols of each of the twelve tribes of Israel on the next page. Cut them out and glue the backs of the sons of Leah to one color of construction paper. Glue the backs of the sons (or grandsons) of Rachel, Zilpah, and Bilhah to different colors of construction paper. Trim the construction paper along the edges of the pictures. With a hole punch put a hole in the top of each picture. Cut 12 foot-long lengths of string. Tie one end of each string to the hole of a picture and the other end to a clothes hanger. Make two paper namecards, one reading Jacob and the other reading Israel. Tape one just under the hook of the hanger. Glue the second namecard to the back of the first.

THE EMBLEMS ON THE STANDARDS OF THE TRIBES.

TWELVE TRIBES OF ISRAEL
Project 3—Rembrandt's "Jacob Blessing the Sons of Joseph"

Rembrandt, Harmensz. van Rijn (1606–1669) is widely regarded as the greatest Dutch artist. He was born at Leiden, studied at the Latin school, and enrolled for a short period at the university before leaving c. 1620 to train as a painter. In 1631 Rembrandt received his first official commission for a formal portrait, from the Amsterdam merchant Nicolaes Ruts.

About this time, Rembrandt moved to Amsterdam and soon established himself as the leading portrait painter of the city. His output in these early years was prodigious. He excelled at highly-finished single portraits, but the ground-breaking work which established his reputation was in making group portraits. In his painting Rembrandt invigorated the tradition by investing his paintings with human drama in a psychologically convincing way, unified by the deep, rich shadows which surround the strategically-illuminated figures.

At this time Rembrandt married Saskia van Uylenburch, the daughter of his wealthy picture-dealer. Rembrandt was evidently devoted to her, painting her on many occasions. In 1639 the couple bought a splendid house in Amsterdam and Rembrandt began to stock it with pictures, prints and all kinds of objects, from armour to old costumes, as prospective props for future paintings. The couple were beset by the tragedy of a succession of infant deaths, culminating in Saskia's death in childbirth in 1642. Only one child lived beyond infancy. Then Rembrandt's financial situation deteriorated during the 1640s and by 1656 he had declared himself insolvent.

From the 1640s onwards formal portraiture formed a smaller percentage of Rembrandt's total output, a change that was been attributed to his grief over the death of Saskia and his weariness of the expressive limitations of the genre. Meanwhile, Rembrandt was exploring the possibilities of religious subjects and landscape. In these years he produced some of his most deeply-felt biblical paintings, like *Jacob Blessing the Sons of Joseph* in 1656. His female nudes are some of the most sympathetic ever painted by a male painter. His technique became broader, more experimental; often he would use the butt-end of his brush to create a desired effect. Rembrandt painted till the end; one of his most moving works, *The Return of the Prodigal Son* dates from the year of his death.

TWELVE TRIBES OF ISRAEL
Project 3, Page 2

Using the artwork on the cover of this manual or the image on the previous page, discuss Rembrandt's Jacob Blessing the Sons of Joseph.

1. Asenath, the wife of Joseph is not mentioned in the biblical account of this event but is in the painting. Why might have Rembrandt included her?

   _____

   _____

2. Why are Joseph and Asenath dressed like royalty?

   _____

   _____

3. What time period is their clothing from?

   _____

   _____

4. Why would the artist paint them in clothes other than what would be historically accurate?

   _____

   _____

5. What biblical event is being alluded to by Joseph's father wearing an animal skin?

   _____

   _____

6. What is in the center of the painting and why?

   _____

   _____

TWELVE TRIBES OF ISRAEL
Test

1. What is the date for the twelve tribes of Israel?

   _____

   _____

2. What is the Scripture reference for the twelve tribes of Israel?

   _____

   _____

3. What had God promised to Abraham?

   _____

   _____

   _____

4. What are Abraham, Isaac, and Jacob known as?

   _____

   _____

   _____

5. God changed _____ name to _____.

6. Jacob had _____ sons and they became _____

7. What are the descendants of Jacob's sons known as?

   _____

   _____

   _____

TWELVE TRIBES OF ISRAEL
Test, Page 2

Review

1. In what disguise did Satan come to tempt Eve?

   _____

   _____

   _____

2. Who was so righteous that God did not allow him to see death?

   _____

   _____

3. Who participated in the first covenant that is described in the Bible?

   _____

   _____

4. Why did Lot's wife turn into a pillar of salt?

   _____

   _____

   _____

5. Whom did Isaac marry?

   _____

   _____

6. For what did Esau agree to sell his birthright?

   _____

   _____

Twelve Tribes of Israel
Test, Page 3

7. List all of the titles and Scripture references studied so far.

MOSES' BIRTH
Worksheet

1. What is the date for the birth of Moses?

   _____

   _____

2. What is the Scripture reference for the birth of Moses?

   _____

   _____

3. What did the new Pharaoh fear about the Israelites?

   _____

   _____

   _____

4. What did Pharaoh do to the Israelites?

   _____

   _____

   _____

5. What did Pharaoh order the midwives to do?

   _____

   _____

   _____

6. What did the Levite couple do to save their son?

   _____

   _____

   _____

MOSES' BIRTH
Worksheet, Page 2

7. Who found the Levite baby?

_____

_____

_____

_____

8. What does the name Moses mean?

_____

_____

_____

_____

MOSES' BIRTH
Project 1—Bible Reading

*Read the acount of Moses' birth in Exodus,
then fill in the crossword puzzle below.*

Across

2. Pharaoh ordered them to kill Israelite boys
   when they were born.

4. Moses was put in a basket in the _____ River.

5. Moses' _____ hid along the river to watch the baby.

7. The _____ of Pharaoh found the baby in the river.

8. Moses' own mother was paid to _____
   him for the princess.

Down

1. Pharaoh feared the numerous Israelites
   so he made them _____.

2. The name _____ means "to draw out".

3. Moses' parents were from the tribe of _____.

6. Egyptian women were _____ in the river near the basket.

MOSES' BIRTH
Project 2—Baby book page

A baby book is a great way to record events and memories in the life of a child. Maybe you have a baby book that you enjoy reading since you don't remember for yourself your earliest years. Assume you are completing a baby book for Moses. Fill in the page below from a baby book as if you were a parent of Moses. Some answers require strict accuracy to what is written in Exodus 1-2:10. The last two answers may allow for some creativity that is consistent with what is listed in the Bible.

When I Was Born . . .

I was born in the country of _____

What was going on in the land at that time _____

My parents' nationality was _____

They were from the tribe of _____

My Mom's reaction when she saw me was _____

I was named _____ which means _____

When I Was Growing Up . . .

I took an unusual trip _____

The house I grew up in was _____

My days were filled with _____

Moses' Birth
Test

1. What is the date for the birth of Moses?

   _____

   _____

2. What is the Scripture reference for the birth of Moses?

   _____

   _____

3. A new pharaoh made the Israelites slaves because

   _____

   _____

   _____

4. The _____ were ordered by Pharaoh to kill all

   _____ when they were born.

   They feared _____ so they did not obey Pharaoh.

5. From what Hebrew tribe was Moses?

   _____

   _____

6. How was Moses saved?

   _____

   _____

   _____

7. Who found baby Moses?

   _____

   _____

   _____

   _____

MOSES' BIRTH
Test, Page 2

8. Who was hiding in the reeds to see what happened to Moses?

_____

_____

_____

_____

9. Who nursed Moses?

_____

_____

_____

Review

1. What was Noah to take into the ark with him?

_____

_____

_____

2. What did God promise to Abraham?

_____

_____

_____

_____

3. Why did Abraham marry Hagar?

_____

_____

_____

_____

MOSES' BIRTH
Test, Page 3

4. How was Rebekah related to Isaac? (other than being his wife)

   _____

   _____

5. What did Jacob do so that Isaac would think he was giving the blessing to Esau?

   _____

   _____

   _____

   _____

6. What did Joseph's brothers do so that their father would think Joseph was dead?

   _____

   _____

   _____

   _____

MOSES' BIRTH
Test, Page 4

7. List all of the titles and Scripture references studied so far.

_____

_____

_____

_____

_____

_____

_____

_____

_____

_____

_____

_____

_____

_____

_____

_____

PLAGUES IN EGYPT
Worksheet

1. What is the date for the Plagues in Egypt?

   _____

   _____

2. What is the Scripture reference for the Plagues in Egypt?

   _____

   _____

   _____

3. Through what did God speak to Moses?

   _____

   _____

   _____

4. What did God tell Moses to do for the Israelites?

   _____

   _____

   _____

   _____

5. Who went with Moses to Pharaoh?

   _____

   _____

   _____

6. What did Moses request from Pharaoh?

   _____

   _____

   _____

   _____

PLAGUES IN EGYPT
Worksheet, Page 2

7. What did God send each time Pharaoh refused Moses' request?

_____

_____

_____

_____

8. Each plague was an attack on what?

_____

_____

_____

_____

1. ATHOR 2. PTAH 3. ISIS 4. OSIRIS 5. NEITH 6. BUBASTIS 7. APIS 8. BEG 9. IBIS 10. SHAU 11. SCARABAEUS

Plagues in Egypt
Project 1—Bible Reading

Read Exodus 3 and write a paragraph explaining Moses' experience with the burning bush.

_____

_____

_____

_____

_____

_____

_____

_____

_____

_____

_____

_____

_____

_____

_____

_____

_____

_____

_____

_____

_____

PLAGUES IN EGYPT
Project 2

It took Pharaoh quite a bit of convincing to let the Israelites go. But when God was through with him he had good reason— ten of them! Make a poster illustrating the top ten reasons the Israelites should be freed. Cut out the Poster title below (or make your own) and paste it to another sheet of paper. All around the title, illustrate and label each reason why the Israelites should go. Each plague would have been another reason to get rid of the Israelites. You may number the plagues in the order in which they occurred. Or you may number the first plague as number ten and count down to the number one reason—the killing of the firstborn.

PLAGUES IN EGYPT
Test

1. What is the date for the Plagues in Egypt?

   _____

   _____

2. What is the Scripture reference for the Plagues in Egypt?

   _____

   _____

3. God spoke to Moses through a _____ and called him to

   _____ .

4. What did Moses request of Pharaoh?

   _____

   _____

   _____

5. Who went with Moses to Pharaoh?

   _____

   _____

   _____

6. How many times did Moses go to Pharaoh?

   _____

   _____

   _____

7. Each time Pharaoh refused, God sent a _____ which was a

   direct attack on _____ .

PLAGUES IN EGYPT
Test, Page 2

Review

1. Who lived to be 969 years old?

   _____

   _____

2. Why was it miraculous for Sarah and Abraham to have a child?

   _____

   _____

3. Who were the twin sons of Isaac and Rebekah?

   _____

   _____

4. Why were Joseph's brothers jealous of him?

   _____

   _____

   _____

5. Who was the Egyptian to whom Joseph became a slave?

   _____

   _____

   _____

6. What did Joseph tell Pharaoh that his dreams meant?

   _____

   _____

   _____

   _____

PLAGUES IN EGYPT
Test, Page 3

7. List all of the titles and Scripture references studied so far.

_____

_____

_____

_____

_____

_____

_____

_____

_____

_____

_____

_____

_____

_____

_____

_____

_____

THE EXODUS
Worksheet

1. What is the date for the Exodus?

   _____

   _____

2. What is the Scripture reference for the Exodus?

   _____

   _____

3. What was the tenth plague on Egypt?

   _____

   _____

4. How were the Israelites spared from the tenth plague?

   _____

   _____

   _____

5. What special day of the Israelites remembered God's sparing them from the tenth plague?

   _____

   _____

   _____

6. Where did the Israelites camp after leaving Egypt?

   _____

   _____

   _____

THE EXODUS
Worksheet, Page 2

7. What did Pharaoh do when he changed his mind?

_____

_____

_____

_____

8. How did God save the Israelites from the Egyptians?

_____

_____

_____

_____

_____

THE EXODUS
Project 1—Bible Reading

Read the account of the Red Sea crossing in Exodus 14. Use each phrase below in a sentence that relates to this story. For example: . . .silver, gold, and clothing. . . The Israelites left Egypt taking along Egyptian silver, gold, and clothing.

. . . pursued the Israelites . . .

_____

_____

_____

. . . camping by the sea . . .

_____

_____

_____

. . . stretched out his hands . . .

_____

_____

_____

. . . pillar of cloud . . .

_____

_____

_____

. . . chariots and horsemen . . .

_____

_____

_____

THE EXODUS
Project 2—Diorama

Supplies

Clay or play dough—blue, brown, and green

Sand

1 ft. square piece of cardboard

1 ft. square piece of posterboard

paper people and chariot cutouts

Directions

Have students make a diorama depicting the parting of the Red Sea. They may choose any part of the crossing to depict. Form clay into the parted waters on top of the cardboard square. Students may want to make ground from clay and/or sand on either side of their Red Sea. Have students color the paper cutouts, glue to posterboard then cut out. Place them on the diorama.

THE EXODUS
Project 2—Diorama, Page 2

THE EXODUS
Test

1. What is the date for the Exodus?

   _____

   _____

2. What is the Scripture reference for the Exodus?

   _____

   _____

3. After how many plagues did Pharaoh let the Israelites leave?

   _____

   _____

   _____

4. Describe the last plague on Egypt?

   _____

   _____

   _____

   _____

   _____

5. What did the Israelites put on their doorposts to be spared from the last plague?

   _____

   _____

   _____

6. By what sea were the Israelites trapped by Pharaoh's men?

   _____

   _____

   _____

The Exodus
Test, Page 2

7. How did God save the Israelites from the Egyptians?

_____

_____

_____

_____

8. What happened to the Egyptian army?

_____

_____

_____

Review

1. Why was Jacob given a name which means "grabber"?

_____

_____

_____

2. Put the following names in the order in which they lived: *Jacob, Isaac, Joseph, Abraham*

_____

_____

_____

_____

3. What caused Joseph's brothers to come to Egypt?

_____

_____

_____

THE EXODUS
Test, Page 3

4. List all of the titles and Scripture references studied so far.

_____

_____

_____

_____

_____

_____

_____

_____

_____

_____

_____

_____

_____

_____

_____

_____

_____

_____

_____

_____

THE TEN COMMANDMENTS
Worksheet

1. What is the date for the Ten Commandments?

   _____

   _____

2. What is the Scripture reference for the Ten Commandments?

   _____

   _____

3. What did God give to Moses on Mt. Sinai?

   _____

   _____

   _____

4. On what were the ten commandments written?

   _____

   _____

5. List the Ten Commandments in order.

   1. _____

   _____

   2. _____

   _____

   3. _____

   _____

   4. _____

   _____

   5. _____

   _____

THE TEN COMMANDMENTS
Worksheet, Page 2

6. _____

_____

7. _____

_____

8. _____

_____

9. _____

_____

10. _____

_____

TEN COMMANDMENTS
Project 1—Bible Reading

Read in Exodus 19 about how the Israelites gathered at Mt. Sinai before he gave them the Ten Commandments. Then fill in the words below that complete the sentences. Use the number of blanks to help you find the correct answer.

1. The people consecrated themselves and washed their _ _ _ _ _ _ _ _ . (Ex. 19:10)

2. Moses was to set _ _ _ _ _ _ _ around the mountain,

   and no one was to _ _ _ _ _ it. (Ex. 19:12)

3. On the third day a thick _ _ _ _ _ _ was on the mountain. (Ex. 19:16)

4. Mt. Sinai was all in _ _ _ _ _ _ , because the Lord descended upon it in

   _ _ _ _ _ . The whole mountain _ _ _ _ _ _ _ . (Ex. 19:18)

Moses was up on Mt. Sinai for 40 days when God was giving him the Ten Commandments. While Israel was camped at Mt. Sinai, God gave them laws and guidelines other than the Ten Commandments.

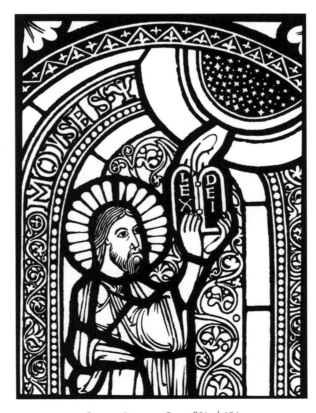

TEN COMMANDMENTS
Project 2

Have students familiarize themselves with the *Westminster Shorter Catechism* on the next page as well as the depth of meaning in the Ten Commandments with this project. On a large sheet of butcher paper write the headings of Commandments, WHAT IS REQUIRED, and WHAT IS FORBIDDEN (about 9 inches apart). Students will cut out the boxes below. Arrange the commandments in order under the Commandments column. Read each box one at a time and try to determine which commandment it is explaining. Put each box in the row of the commandment that it explains and under the column of WHAT IS REQUIRED or WHAT IS FORBIDDEN. You may wish to give the students a copy of the *Westminster Shorter Catechism* section provided after they have attempted to determine where each box belongs on the chart. When students have correctly placed each box, they may glue the boxes to the butcher paper and draw lines to separate the columns and rows.

You shall not murder.

You shall not bear false witness against your neighbor.

You shall not take the name of the Lord your God in vain.

Honor your father and mother.

You shall have no other gods before me.

You shall not steal.

Remember the Sabbath day to keep it holy.

You shall not commit adultery.

You shall not covet.

You shall not make for yourself a carved image.

TEN COMMANDMENTS
Project 2, Page 2

Westminster Shorter Catechism QUESTIONS 42–82

Q. 42. What is the sum of the ten commandments?
A. The sum of the ten commandments is, To love the Lord our God with all our heart, with all our soul, with all our strength, and with all our mind; and our neighbour as ourselves.[1]

Q. 43. What is the preface to the ten commandments?
A. The preface to the ten commandments is in these words, I am the Lord thy God, which have brought thee out of the land of Egypt, out of the house of bondage.[2]

Q. 44. What doth the preface to the ten commandments teach us?
A. The preface to the ten commandments teacheth us, That because God is the Lord, and our God, and Redeemer, therefore we are bound to keep all his commandments.[3]

Q. 45. Which is the first commandment?
A. The first commandment is, Thou shalt have no other gods before me.[4]

Q. 46. What is required in the first commandment?
A. The first commandment requireth us to know and acknowledge God to be the only true God, and our God,[5] and to worship and glorify him accordingly.[6]

Q. 47. What is forbidden in the first commandment?
A. The first commandment forbiddeth the denying,[7] or not worshipping and glorifying the true God as God,[8] and our God;[9] and the giving of that worship and glory to any other, which is due to him alone.[10]

Q. 48. What are we specially taught by these words [before me] in the first commandment?
A. These words [before me] in the first commandment teach us, That God, who seeth all things, taketh notice of, and is much displeased with, the sin of having any other god.[11]

Q. 49. Which is the second commandment?
A. The second commandment is, Thou shalt not make unto thee any graven image, or any liheness of any thing that is in heaven above, or that is in the earth beneath, or that is in the water under the earth: thou shalt not bow down thyself to them, nor serve them: for I the Lord thy God am a jealous God, visiting the iniquity of the fathers upon the children unto the third and fourth generation of them that hate me; and shewing mercy unto thousands of them that love me, and keep my commandments.[12]

Q. 50. What is required in the second commandment?
A. The second commandment requireth the receiving, observing, and keeping pure and entire, all such religious worship and ordinances as God hath appointed in his word.[13]

Q. 51. What is forbidden in the second commandment?
A. The second commandment forbiddeth the worshipping of God by images,[14] or any other way not appointed in his words.

Q. 52. What are the reasons annexed to the second commandment?
A. The reasons annexed to the second commandment are, God's sovereignty over us,[15] his propriety in us,[16] and the zeal he hath to his own worship.[17]

TEN COMMANDMENTS
Project 2, Page 3

Q. 53. Which is the third commandment?
A. The third commandment is, Thou shalt not take the name of the Lord thy God in vain: for the Lord will not hold him guiltless that taketh his name in vain.[18]

Q. 54. What is required in the third commandment?
A. The third commandment requireth the holy and reverent use of God's names,[19] titles,[20] attributes,[21] ordinances,[22] word[23] and works.[24]

Q. 55. What is forbidden in the third commandment?
A. The third commandment forbiddeth all profaning or abusing of any thing whereby God maketh himself known.[25]

Q. 56. What is the reason annexed to the third commandment?
A. The reason annexed to the third commandment is, That however the breakers of this commandment may escape punishment from men, yet the Lord our God will not suffer them to escape his righteous judgment.[26]

Q. 57. Which is the fourth commandment?
A. The fourth commandment is, Remember the sabbath day, to keep it holy. Six days shalt thou, labour, and do all thy work: but the seventh day is the sabbath of the Lord thy God: in it thou shalt not do any work, thou, nor thy son, nor thy daughter, thy man-servant, nor thy maid-servant, nor thy cattle, nor thy stranger that is within thy gates: for in six days the Lord made heaven and earth, the sea, and all that in them is, and rested the seventh day: wherefore the Lord blessed the sabbath-day, and hallowed it.[27]

Q. 58. What is required in the fourth commandment?
A. The fourth commandment requireth the keeping holy to God such set times as he hath appointed in his word; expressly one whole day in seven, to be a holy sabbath to himself.[28]

Q. 59. Which day of the seven hath God appointed to be the weekly sabbath?
A. From the beginning of the world to the resurrection of Christ, God appointed the seventh day of the week to be the weekly sabbath; and the first day of the week ever since, to continue to the end of the world, which is the Christian sabbath.[29]

Q. 60. How is the sabbath to be sanctified?
A. The sabbath is to be sanctified by a holy resting all that day,[30] even from such worldly employments and recreations as are lawful on other days;[31] and spending the whole time in the public[32] and private exercises of God's worship,[33] except so much as is to be taken up in the works of necessity and mercy.[34]

Q. 61. What is forbidden in the fourth commandment?
A. The fourth commandment forbiddeth the omission or careless performance of the duties required,[35] and the profaning the day by idleness,[36] or doing that which is in itself sinful,[37] or by unnecessary thoughts, words, or works, about our worldly employments or recreations.[38]

Q. 62. What are the reasons annexed to the fourth commandment?
A. The reasons annexed to the fourth commandment are, God's allowing us six days of the week for our own employments,[39] his challenging a special propriety in the seventh, his own example, and his blessing the sabbath day.[40]

TEN COMMANDMENTS
Project 2, Page 4

Q. 63. Which is the fifth commandment?
A. The fifth commandment is, Honour thy father and thy mother; that thy days may be long upon the land which the Lord thy God giveth thee.[41]

Q. 64. What is required in the fifth commandment?
A. The fifth commandment requireth the preserving the honour, and performing the duties, belonging to every one in their several places and relations, as superiors,[42] inferiors[43] or equals.[44]

Q. 65. What is forbidden in the fifth commandment?
A. The fifth commandment forbiddeth the neglecting of, or doing any thing against, the honour and duty which belongeth to every one in their several places and relations.[45]

Q. 66. What is the reason annexed to the fifth commandment?
A. The reason annexed to the fifth commandment, is a promise of long life and prosperity (as far as it shall serve for God's glory and their own good) to all such as keep this commandment.[46]

Q. 67. Which is the sixth commandment?
A. The sixth commandment is, Thou shalt not kill.[47]

Q. 68. What is required in the sixth commandment?
A. The sixth commandment requireth all lawful endeavours to preserve our own life,[48] and the life of others.[49]

Q. 69. What is forbidden in the sixth commandment?
A. The sixth commandment forbiddeth the taking away of our own life, or the life of our neighbour unjustly, or whatsoever tendeth thereunto.[50]

Q. 70. Which is the seventh commandment?
A. The seventh commandment is, Thou shalt not commit adultery.[51]

Q. 71. What is required in the seventh commandment?
A. The seventh commandment requireth the preservation of our own and our neighbour's chastity, in heart, speech, and behaviour.[52]

Q. 72. What is forbidden in the seventh commandment?
A. The seventh commandment forbiddeth all unchaste thoughts, words, and actions.[53]

Q. 73. Which is the eighth commandment?
A. The eighth commandment is, Thou shalt not steal.[54]

Q. 74. What is required in the eighth commandment?
A. The eighth commandment requireth the lawful procuring and furthering the wealth and outward estate of ourselves and others.[55]

Q. 75. What is forbidden in the eighth commandment?
A. The eighth commandment forbiddeth whatsoever doth or may unjustly hinder our own or our neighbour's wealth or outward estate.[56]

Q. 76. Which is the ninth commandment?
A. The ninth commandment is, Thou shalt not bear false witness against thy neighbour.[57]

TEN COMMANDMENTS
Project 2, Page 5

Q. 77. What is required in the ninth commandment?
A. The ninth commandment requireth the maintaining and promoting of truth between man and man,[58] and of our own and our neighbour's good name,[59] especially in witness-bearing.[60]

Q. 78. What is forbidden in the ninth commandment?
A. The ninth commandment forbiddeth whatsoever is prejudicial to truth, or injurious to our own or our neighbour's good name.[61]

Q. 79. Which is the tenth commandment?
A. The tenth commandment is, Thou shalt not covet thy neighbour's house, thou shalt not covet thy neighbour's wife, nor his man-servant, nor his maid-servant, nor his ox, nor his ass, nor any thing that is thy neighbour's.[62]

Q. 80. What is required in the tenth commandment?
A. The tenth commandment requireth full contentment with our own conditions, with a right and charitable frame of spirit toward our neighbour, and all that is his.[63]

Q. 81. What is forbidden in the tenth commandment?
A. The tenth commandment forbiddeth all discontentment with our own estate,[64] envying or grieving at the good of our neighbour,[65] and all inordinate motions and affections to any thing that is his.[66]

Q. 82. Is any man able perfectly to keep the commandments of God?
A. No mere man since the fall is able in this life perfectly to keep the commandments of God,[67] but doth daily break them in thought, word, and deed.[68]

Westminster Shorter Catechism
SCRIPTURAL REFERENCE

[1]Matt. 22:37-40
[2]Exod. 20:2
[3]Luke 1:74,75; 1 Pet. 1:15-19
[4]Exod. 20:3
[5]1 Chron. 28:9; Deut. 26:17
[6]Matt.4:10; Ps. 29:2
[7]Ps. 14:1 1 Rom. 1:21
[8]Ps. 81:10,11
[9]Rom. 1:25
[10]Ezek. 8:5,6; Ps. 96:20,21
[11]Exod. 20:4-6.
[12]Deut. 32:46; Matt. 28:20; Acts. 2:42
[13]Deut. 4:15-19; Exod. 32:5,8
[14]Deut. 12:31,32
[15]Ps. 95:2,3,6
[16]Ps. 45:11
[17]Exod. 34:13,14
[18]Exod. 20:7
[19]Matt. 6:9; Deut. 28:58
[20]Ps. 68:4
[21]Rev. 15:3,4
[22]Mal. 1:11,14
[23]Ps. 138:1,2
[24]Job 36:24
[25]Mal. 1:6,7,12; Mal.2:2; Mal. 3:14
[26]1 Sam. 2:12,17,22,29; 1 Sam. 3:13; Deut. 28:58,59
[27]Exod. 20:8-11
[28]Deut. 5:12-14
[29]Gen. 2:2,3; 1 Cor. 16:1,2; Acts 20:7
[30]Exod. 20:8,10; Exod. 16:25-28
[31]Neh. 13:15-22
[32]Luke 4:16; Acts 20:7; Ps. 92:title; Isa. 66:23
[33]Matt. 12:1-31
[34]Ezek. 22:26; Amos 8:5; Mal. 1:13
[35]Acts 20:7,9
[36]Ezek. 23:38
[37]Jer. 17:24-26; Isa. 58:13

[38]Exod. 20:9
[39]Exod. 20:11
[40]Exod. 20:12
[41]Eph. 5:21
[42]1 Pet. 2:17
[43]Rom. 12:10
[44]Matt. 15:46; Ezek. 34:2-4; Rom. 13:8
[45]Deut. 5:16; Eph. 6:2,3
[46]Exod. 20:13
[47]Eph. 5:28,29
[48]1 Kings 18:4
[49]Acts 16:28
[50]Exod. 20:14
[51]1 Cor. 7:2,3,5,34,36; Col. 4:6; 1 Pet. 3:2
[52]Matt. 15:19; Matt. 5:28; Eph. 5:3,4
[53]Exod. 20:15
[54]Gen. 30:30; 1 Tim. 5:8; Lev. 25:35; Deut. 22:1-5; Exod. 23:4,5; Gen. 47:14,20
[55]Prov. 21:17; Prov. 23:20,21; Prov. 28:19; Eph. 4:28
[56]Exod. 20:16
[57]Zech. 8:16
[58]3 John 12
[59]Prov. 14:5,25
[60]1 Sam. 17:28
[61]Exod. 20:17
[62]Heb. 13:5; 1 Tim. 6:6
[63]Job 31:29; Rom. 12:15; 1 Tim. 1:5; 1 Cor. 13:4-7
[64]1 Kings 21:4; Esther5:13; 1 Cor. 10:10
[65]Gal. 5:26; James 3:14,16
[66]Rom. 7:7,8; Rom. 13:9; Deut. 5:21
[67]Eccl. 7:20; 1 John 1:8,10; Gal. 5:17
[68]Gen. 6:5; Gen. 8:21; Rom. 3:9-21; James 3:2-13

TEN COMMANDMENTS
Project 2, Page 6

the preservation of our own and our neighbor's chastity,
in heart, speech, and behavior

the neglecting of or doing anything against, the honor and duty which
belongeth to everyone in their several places and relations

requireth the keeping holy to God such set times as he hath appointed in his
word; expressly one whole day in seven, to be a holy sabbath to himself

profaning or abusing of anything whereby God maketh himself known

the taking away of our own life, and the life of others

to know and acknowledge God to be the only true God, and our God,
and to worship and glorify him accordingly

the maintaining and promoting of truth between man and man, and our own
and our neighbor's good name, especially in witness-bearing

all lawful endeavors to preserve our own life, and the life of others

the worshipping of God by images, or any other way not appointed in his word

the holy and reverent use of all God's names, titles, attributes,
ordinances, Word, and works

all discontentment with our own estate, envying or grieving at the good of our
neighbor, and all inordinate emotions and affections to anything that is his

TEN COMMANDMENTS
Project 2, Page 7

preserving the honor, and performing the duties, belonging to everyone in their several places and relations, as superiors, inferiors, or equals

the lawful procuring and furthering the wealth and outward estate of ourselves and others

all unchaste thoughts, words, and actions

full contentment with our own condition, with a right and charitable frame of spirit toward our neighbor and all that is his

the denying, or not worshipping and glorifying, the true God as God, and our God; and the giving of that worship and glory to any other which is due to him alone

the omission, or careless performance, of the duties required, and the profaning the day by idleness, or doing that which is in itself sinful, or by unnecessary thoughts, words, or works, about our worldly employments or recreations

whatsoever doth, or may, unjustly hinder our own, or our neighbor's, wealth or outward estate

whatsoever is prejudicial to truth, or injurious to our own or our neighbor's good name

the receiving, observing, and keeping pure and entire all such religious worship and ordinances as God hath appointed in his Word

THE TEN COMMANDMENTS
Test

1. What is the date for the Ten Commandments?

   _____

   _____

2. What is the Scripture reference for the Ten Commandments?

   _____

   _____

3. On what mountain did God give Moses the Ten Commandments?

   _____

   _____

4. Who wrote the Ten Commandments?

   _____

   _____

5. The Ten Commandments:

   1. You shall have _____.

   2. You shall not make_____.

   3. You shall not take _____.

   4. Remember _____.

   5. Honor _____.

   6. You shall not _____.

   7. You shall not _____.

   8. You shall not _____.

   9. You shall not _____.

   10. You shall not _____.

TEN COMMANDMENTS
Test, Page 2

Review

1. What was Abraham's name before God made his covenant with him?

   _____

   _____

2. What did God command Abraham to do to Isaac on Mt. Moriah?

   _____

   _____

   _____

3. Whom did Abraham send to find a wife for Isaac?

   _____

4. How many sons did Jacob have?

   _____

   _____

   _____

5. What did Pharaoh order the Hebrew midwives to do?

   _____

   _____

   _____

Ten Commandments
Test, Page 3

6. List all of the titles and Scripture references studied so far.

Aaron and the Golden Calf
Worksheet

1. What is the date for this card?

    _____

    _____

2. What is the Scripture reference for this card?

    _____

    _____

3. What did the Israelites ask Aaron to do?

    _____

    _____

    _____

4. What did God want to do because of the sin of the Israelites?

    _____

    _____

    _____

5. What did Moses do when he came down the mountain and saw the golden calf?

    _____

    _____

    _____

6. What did Moses' actions show?

    _____

    _____

    _____

AARON AND THE GOLDEN CALF
Worksheet, Page 2

7. How did Moses act as a mediator between God and the people?

   _____

   _____

   _____

8. How is Moses like Jesus?

   _____

   _____

   _____

Aaron and the Golden Calf
Project 1—Bible Reading

Read Exodus 32 and answer the following questions as you read. What did the people think might have happened to Moses up on the mountain? From where did the Israelites get the gold to make the calf? What kinds of things did the people do on the day of the feast? What did Joshua think was going on in the camp?

Now write a paragraph telling what happened when Moses came down the mountain. Be sure to include what happened to the tablets and the golden calf. Also include what was the people's punishment.

_____

_____

_____

_____

_____

_____

_____

_____

_____

_____

_____

Aaron and the Golden Calf
Project 2—Drama

Students can really remember that which they explain or act out. Assign students parts as suggested below. Allow the students to come up with the dialog from their own knowledge of the story. It is suggested that the story be acted out several times. Switch parts each time.

Cast of Characters:

Aaron

Moses

Voice of God

Golden Calf

Israelites

Aaron and the Golden Calf
Test

1. What is the date for this card?

   _____

   _____

2. What is the Scripture reference for this card?

   _____

   _____

3. What did the Israelites really want?

   _____

   _____

   _____

4. What did the Israelites ask Aaron to do?

   _____

   _____

5. How did Moses respond when he saw the golden calf?

   _____

   _____

   _____

6. What did Moses' actions show?

   _____

   _____

   _____

7. What other man in the Bible stood between God and his people to turn away God's wrath?

   _____

   _____

Review

1. Put the brothers together. Put the oldest brother first. Jacob, Cain, Abel, Esau

   _____ and _____

   _____ and _____

2. Who stopped Abraham from sacrificing Isaac?

   _____

   _____

   _____

3. How did Joseph end up in prison?

   _____

   _____

   _____

4. Why did Pharaoh place Joseph second in command in Egypt?

   _____

   _____

   _____

5. List all of the titles and Scripture references studied so far.

   _____

   _____

   _____

   _____

   _____

   _____

Aaron and the Golden Calf
Test, Page 3

5. (continued)

_____

_____

_____

_____

_____

_____

_____

_____

_____

_____

_____

_____

_____

_____

_____

_____

MOSES GETS NEW TABLETS
Worksheet

1. What is the date of Moses Gets New Tablets?

   _____

   _____

2. What is the Scripture reference for Moses Gets New Tablets?

   _____

   _____

3. What did God have Moses make?

   _____

   _____

   _____

MOSES GETS NEW TABLETS
Worksheet, Page 2

4. The Israelites were described as stiff-necked like _____.

5. What did God warn the Israelites not to do?

   _____

   _____

   _____

6. What was to happen to the firstborn animals?

   _____

   _____

   _____

7. How long was Moses on the mountain?

   _____

   _____

   _____

8. What was strange about Moses when he came back down?

   _____

   _____

   _____

9. What did Moses have to wear after he came down the mountain?

   _____

   _____

   _____

Moses Gets New Tablets
Project 1—Bible Reading

Read about Moses receiving new tablets in Exodus 34. Unscramble the words below on the left. Then draw a line to connect the words with the phrases on the right that they correctly complete.

Letbats   _____ days

Isain   observe the _____

Frontbirs   new stone _____

Bastbah   no _____ or water

Iftsf-denkec   _____ people

Tryof   on Mt. _____

Bader   covered with a _____

Hinsing   sacrifice the _____

Evil   a _____ face

Moses Gets New Tablets
Project 2

This project will illustrate Moses and Jesus as mediators between God and man.

You will need 2 popsicle sticks and an 11" x 3" strip of paper. Fold the paper in half as shown. Glue each popsicle stick with its top edge flush with the crease. The extra length of the popsicle sticks should stick out from each side of the paper. On the left popsicle stick write *God*, and on the right stick write *Man*.

Fold the top flap down and glue the pictures of Moses and Jesus onto the two flaps as shown below. The students may then color the pictures.

Finally, a note on the illustrations: Often in art Moses is depicted as having horns. This is due to a mistranslation from the 12th century of Exodus 34:50 —instead of saying that Moses' face was "beaming" it was translated as "horned."

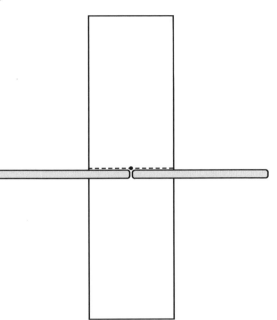

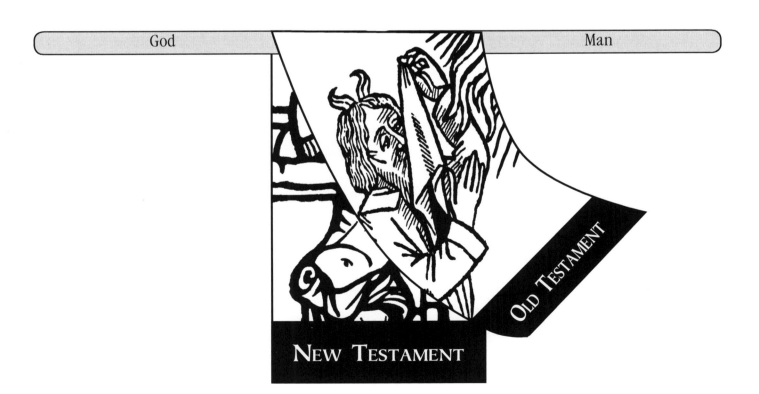

MOSES GETS NEW TABLETS
Project 2, Page 2

OLD TESTAMENT

NEW TESTAMENT

MOSES GETS NEW TABLETS
Test

1. What is the date of Moses Gets New Tablets?

   _____

   _____

2. What is the Scripture reference for Moses Gets New Tablets?

   _____

   _____

3. What was written on the new set of tablets?

   _____

   _____

4. To what mountain did Moses bring the new tablets that God had commanded
   him to make?

   _____

   _____

   _____

5. With whom were the Israelites not to marry or make covenants?

   _____

   _____

   _____

6. What were the Israelites to do with their firstborn animals?

   _____

   _____

   _____

   _____

Moses Gets New Tablets
Test, Page 2

7. Describe Moses' stay on the mountain.

_____

_____

_____

_____

_____

8. What had happened to Moses' face when he came back down?

_____

_____

_____

9. What did Moses have to wear after he came down the mountain?

_____

_____

_____

Review

1. Which son of Adam murdered his brother?

_____

_____

2. What did the angel tell Hagar about her descendants?

_____

_____

_____

MOSES GETS NEW TABLETS
Test, Page 3

3. Name the twelve tribes of Israel.

_____   _____

_____   _____

_____   _____

_____   _____

_____   _____

4. How was Moses saved from being killed?

_____

_____

_____

_____

5. List all of the titles and Scripture references studied so far.

_____

_____

_____

_____

_____

THE TABERNACLE
AND THE ARK OF THE COVENANT
Worksheet

1. What is the date for this card?

    _____

    _____

2. What is the Scripture reference for this card?

    _____

    _____

3. Who were two of the main craftsmen who worked on the tabernacle?

    _____

    _____

THE TABERNACLE
AND THE ARK OF THE COVENANT
Worksheet, Page 2

4. What did Moses have to do since the people were giving so much money for the building of the tabernacle?

   _____

   _____

5. Describe the tabernacle.

   _____

   _____

   _____

   _____

6. Name three things that were in the tabernacle.

   _____

   _____

   _____

7. Describe the ark of the covenant.

   _____

   _____

   _____

8. What did the High Priest do once a year?

   _____

   _____

   _____

9. The things kept in the ark of the covenant all reminded the people of

   God's _____.

THE TABERNACLE
AND THE ARK OF THE COVENANT
Project 1—Bible Reading

Read the description of the Tabernacle and Ark in Exodus 36, 37. Take note of the materials and design. Inside the four circles below are categories for which you will find examples in the Biblical description of the Ark and the Tabernacle. The circles have spaces for 2, 3, or 4 examples of each category. Fill up the circles with examples from the Biblical description. To get you started, there is an example for each circle in the Example box below.

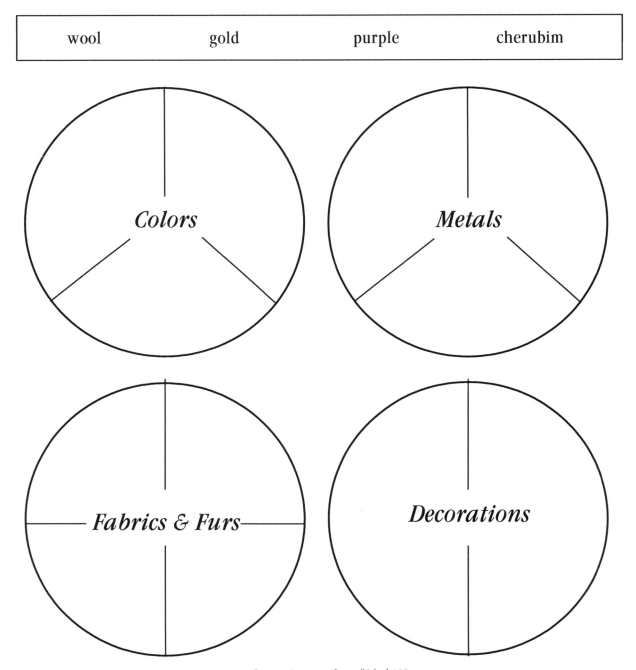

wool   gold   purple   cherubim

Colors

Metals

Fabrics & Furs

Decorations

THE TABERNACLE AND THE ARK OF THE COVENANT

Project 2—Ark of the Covenant Model

Supplies

butter/cream cheese, or similar box

copy of the rings and cherubim from the next page

2 bamboo skewers or dowel rods

gold spray paint

4 plastic push pins

small twig

foam

clay

Directions

Trace and cut out the top of the box on the foam to make the mercy seat. Glue it to the top of the box. Cut out the rings and cherubim. Use a hole punch to remove the center of the rings. Fold along the dotted lines and glue the rings to the side corners of the box as shown in the illustration on the next page. Fold and glue the cherubim to the top of the box as shown. Push the pins into the bottom of the box for the legs. Cut the bamboo skewers or dowel rods 2" longer than the length of the box. Spray paint the box (inside and out) and poles. Form the clay into a jar of manna and the two stone tablets of the Ten Commandments. When the spray paint dries, put the manna, stone tablets, and twig for Aaron's staff inside the ark. Slide the poles through the side rings.

The Tabernacle
and the Ark of the Covenant
Project 2—Ark of the Covenant Model, Page 2

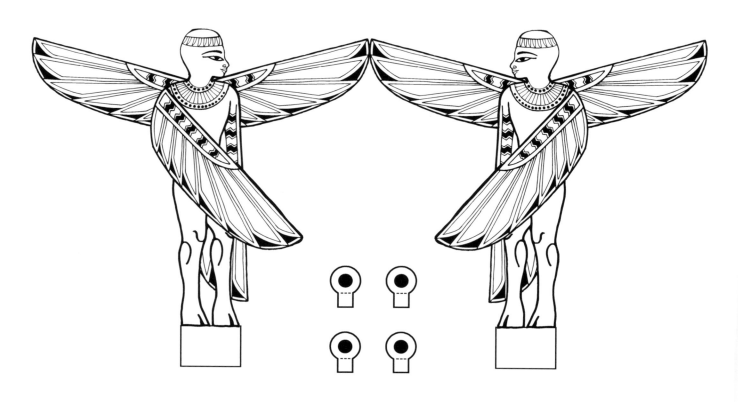

Finished Model

THE TABERNACLE
AND THE ARK OF THE COVENANT
Test

1. What is the date for this card?

   _____

   _____

2. What is the Scripture reference for this card?

   _____

   _____

3. Who were Bezaleel and Aholiab?

   _____

   _____

   _____

4. Name two things that were in the tabernacle.

   _____

   _____

   _____

THE TABERNACLE
AND THE ARK OF THE COVENANT
Test, Page 2

5. The curtain in the tabernacle blocked people off from the _____
_____ Place.

6. What special object was kept behind the curtain?

_____

_____

_____

7. Describe the ark of the covenant.

_____

_____

_____

_____

8. What did the High Priest do once a year?

_____

_____

_____

9. What did the High Priest's actions show the people?

_____

_____

_____

_____

10. Name things kept inside the ark of the covenant to remind the people of God's faithfulness.

_____

_____

THE TABERNACLE
AND THE ARK OF THE COVENANT
Test, Page 3

Review

1. Name two people with whom God made covenants.

_____

_____

_____

2. Where did Reuben convince his brothers that they should put Joseph?

_____

_____

_____

3. Who found Moses and pulled him out of the Nile River?

_____

_____

_____

4. Who came along with Moses to ask Pharaoh to free the Israelites?

_____

_____

_____

5. What did the Israelites place on their doorposts to be spared from the tenth plague?

_____

_____

_____

_____

The Tabernacle
and the Ark of the Covenant
Review, Page 4

6. List all of the titles and Scripture references studied so far.

_____

_____

_____

_____

_____

_____

_____

_____

_____

THE LEVITICAL PRIESTHOOD BEGINS
Worksheet

1. What is the date for this card?

   _____

   _____

2. What is the Scripture reference for this card?

   _____

   _____

3. Who was given the jobs of carrying the tabernacle and helping the sons of Aaron?

   _____

   _____

4. Since there were more firstborns than Levites, what did the people have to do?

   _____

   _____

   _____

5. When the Israelites moved into the Promised Land, why weren't the Levites given any land of their own?

   _____

   _____

   _____

6. What is a priest?

   _____

   _____

   _____

7. Who is our perfect High Priest?

   _____

   _____

BREASTPLATE OF HIGH PRIEST.

THE LEVITICAL PRIESTHOOD BEGINS
Project 1—Bible Reading

Read in Numbers 3 about the beginning of the Levitical priesthood. Complete the word find below, and be sure to know what each word has to do with this event.

```
L E V I S S E R P H A B C D L E
K J I H O F F E R I N G S G A F
L M T N B V C X Z A S D F G M H
L C A M P K C U R T A I N S P J
L P B P O O I U Y T T R E W S W
Q L E V I T E S W E R T Y U T I
I O R P A S D F G H J K L L A Z
Z X N C D V B O B A R K N A N M
I U A Y U U T R U L E W R Q D M
O P C P O I T U S T S O Y T R E
W Q L Q W E R I T A N M N B V C
R S E R V E S E E R W U S Q Z X
T Y Y U I O P L K S J H M G F D
S A Z F I R S T B O R N V B S C
A R O N A A R R O N S A L T E S
T A B E R N A C K L E S L T E R
```

Levites	firstborn	camp	lampstand
serve	ark	offering	altar
tabernacle	duties	curtain	outnumber
	Aaron		

The Levitical Priesthood Begins
Project 2

Read in Exodus 39 about the clothing of a priest. Then color the picture of the priest.

THE LEVITICAL PRIESTHOOD BEGINS
Test

1. What is the date for this card?

   _____

   _____

2. What is the Scripture reference for this card?

   _____

   _____

3. Describe the job of the Levites.

   _____

   _____

   _____

4. When God chose the Levites over the firstborn, why did the people have to give an offering to the Lord?

   _____

   _____

   _____

5. What did the Levites not receive when the Israelites moved into the Promised Land?

   _____

   _____

   _____

6. A _____ is one who stands between God and the people.

7. Why don't we need Levitical priests today?

   _____

   _____

   _____

THE LEVITICAL PRIESTHOOD BEGINS
Test, Page 2

Review

1. What was Abraham willing to do that shows he had faith in God?

   _____

   _____

   _____

2. What is a birthright?

   _____

   _____

   _____

3. How many plagues did God bring on Egypt?

   _____

   _____

4. What Jewish holiday celebrates their being passed over by the angel of death?

   _____

   _____

5. On what mountain did God give Moses the Ten Commandments?

   _____

   _____

THE LEVITICAL PRIESTHOOD BEGINS
Test, Page 3

6. List all of the titles and Scripture references studied so far.

_____

_____

_____

_____

_____

_____

_____

_____

_____

SHOW-BREAD.

THE LEVITICAL PRIESTHOOD BEGINS
Test, Page 4

6. (continued)

_____

_____

_____

_____

_____

_____

_____

_____

_____

_____

_____

_____

_____

_____

_____

THE WILDERNESS WANDERINGS
Worksheet

1. What is the date for Wilderness Wanderings?

   _____

   _____

2. What is the Scripture reference for Wilderness Wanderings?

   _____

   _____

3. How trusting were the Israelites during the
   wilderness wanderings?

   _____

   _____

   _____

4. Fill in the blanks with what God
   provided when they grumbled for
   the following things:

   water _____

   food _____

   meat _____

5. How many spies were sent to scout out the
   land of Canaan?

   _____

   _____

6. How many spies thought they could defeat the Canaanites?

   _____

   _____

THE WILDERNESS WANDERINGS
Worksheet, Page 2

7. How did God punish the Israelites for not believing that God would help them defeat the Canaanites?

_____

_____

_____

8. How did God lead his people through the wilderness?

_____

_____

_____

9. What happened to all of the adults that had not trusted God to enter the Promised Land?

_____

_____

_____

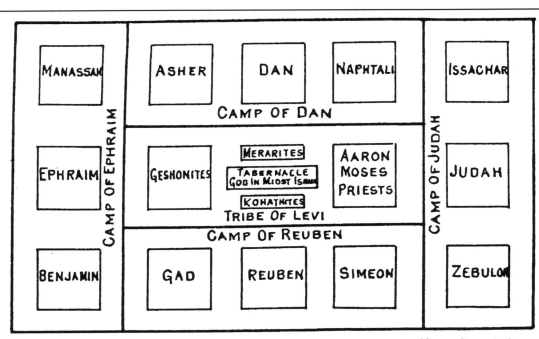

NUM. 2:1 - 3:39

The Wilderness Wanderings
Project 1—Bible Reading

Read in Numbers 13, 14 about the scouting mission in to Canaan and the people's response and consequences. In the space provided below list at least five details or facts that were not printed on your card.

_____

_____

_____

_____

_____

_____

_____

_____

_____

_____

_____

_____

_____

_____

_____

_____

_____

_____

THE WILDERNESS WANDERINGS
Project 2

God led his people through the wilderness with a cloud by day and a pillar of fire by night. At all times the Israelites saw one of these two objects to remind them that God was with them. Color the pictures of the tabernacle below. Make one show daytime with the cloud and the other night with the pillar of fire. Cut out each picture along the dotted lines and glue it to one side of a 3" x 5" notecard. You can use these pictures to remind you of God's constant presence by using it as a bookmark in your Bible. Or punch a hole in the top and hang it in your bedroom.

The Wilderness Wanderings

Project 3—Cartooning

Draw a comic strip illustrating this story. Your comic strip must contain at least four scenes. Use dialog bubbles to include important things that were said.

OUCH! EEP! MUNCH MUNCH ? SPLOOSH !

WILDERNESS WANDERINGS

BACK AT THE CAMP...

TO BE CONTINUED...

THE WILDERNESS WANDERINGS
Test

1. What is the date for Wilderness Wanderings?

   _____

   _____

2. What is the Scripture reference for Wilderness Wanderings?

   _____

   _____

3. Name three things for which the Israelites grumbled.

   _____

   _____

   _____

   _____

4. What were the spies sent out to do?

   _____

   _____

   _____

   _____

5. Which two spies thought they could defeat the Canaanites?

   _____

   _____

6. How did God punish the Israelites for not believing that God would help them defeat the Canaanites?

   _____

   _____

   _____

The Wilderness Wanderings
Test, Page 2

7. What two things did God use to lead his people through the wilderness?

_____

_____

_____

8. What happened to all of the adults that had not trusted God to enter the Promised Land?

_____

_____

_____

Review

1. What did God promise Abraham?

_____

_____

_____

_____

2. Name two Patriarchs.

_____

_____

_____

3. When the Egyptians came after the Israelites when they left Egypt, how did God miraculously save the Israelites?

_____

_____

_____

_____

THE WILDERNESS WANDERINGS
Test, Page 3

4. With what were the Ten Commandments written?

_____

_____

5. What did Moses do when he saw the golden calf?

_____

_____

_____

_____

6. List all of the titles and Scripture references studied so far.

_____

_____

_____

_____

_____

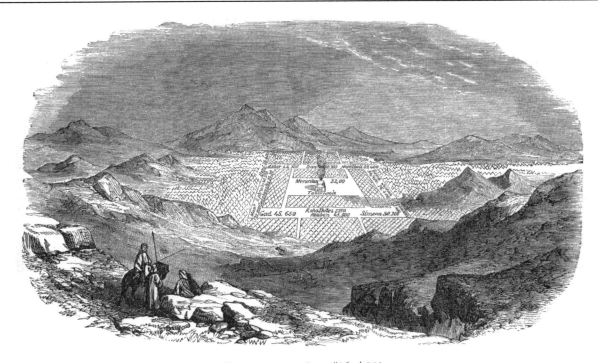

6. (continued)

_____

_____

_____

_____

_____

_____

_____

_____

_____

_____

_____

_____

_____

_____

_____

_____

_____

_____

_____

_____

BALAAM AND HIS DONKEY
Worksheet

1. What is the date for this card?

   _____

   _____

2. What is the Scripture reference for this card?

   _____

   _____

3. Why did the Moabites fear Israel?

   _____

   _____

   _____

   _____

4. Who did the Moabites hire to curse Israel?

   _____

   _____

   _____

   _____

BALAAM AND HIS DONKEY
Worksheet, Page 2

5. Describe Balaam.

_____

_____

_____

_____

6. What did God put in Balaam's path?

_____

_____

7. Why did Balaam's donkey go off the road and then sit down?

_____

_____

_____

_____

8. What miraculous power did God give the donkey?

_____

_____

_____

9. What happened when Balaam tried to curse the Israelites?

_____

_____

_____

_____

BALAAM AND HIS DONKEY
Project 1—Bible Reading

Read in Numbers 22-24 about Balaam, Balak, and the donkey. Using your Bible, find who said each quote below. Write their name in the blank. The quotes are listed in the order in which they are found in the story.

1. _____ "Look, a people has come from Egypt. See, they cover the face of the earth, and are settling next to me!"

2. _____ "If the men come to call you, rise and go with them, but only the word which I speak to you—that you shall do."

3. _____ "What have I done to you that you have struck me these three times?"

4. _____ "I have sinned, for I did not know You stood in the way against me. Now therefore, if it displeases You, I will turn back."

5. _____ "What have you done to me? I took you to curse my enemies, and look, you have blessed them bountifully!"

6. _____ "Did I not tell you, saying, "All that the Lord speaks, that I must do?"

BALAAM AND HIS DONKEY
Project 2—Pin the Words on the Donkey

Play a variation on "Pin the Tail on the Donkey" with words that Balaam's donkey said. Paste the pictures of Balaam, Balak, and the donkey to a large piece of butcher paper. Photocopy and cut out a set of the three quotes for each player. Put a tape doughnut on the back of each quote. Blindfold one player. Read the player a quote and have them try to place it at the mouth of the one that said it. Let them try to correctly place all three quotes. A player wins if he touches the pointed corner of each quote with the mouth who said it.

Balaam and his Donkey
Project 2—Balaam

Balaam and his Donkey
Project 2— Balaam's Donkey

BALAAM AND HIS DONKEY
Project 2—Balak

BALAAM AND HIS DONKEY
Test

1. What is the date for this card?

   _____

   _____

2. What is the Scripture reference for this card?

   _____

   _____

3. Why did the Moabites fear Israel?

   _____

   _____

   _____

4. Why did the Moabites hire Balaam?

   _____

   _____

   _____

5. Describe Balaam.

   _____

   _____

   _____

   _____

6. Why did God send an angel into Balaam's path?

   _____

   _____

   _____

BALAAM AND HIS DONKEY
Test, Page 2

7. What did Balaam's donkey do when it saw the angel?

_____

_____

_____

8. What miraculous power did God give the donkey?

_____

_____

_____

9. What happened when Balaam tried to curse the Israelites?

_____

_____

_____

Review

1. List the ten commandments.

    1. _____

    2. _____

    3. _____

    4. _____

    5. _____

    6. _____

    7. _____

    8. _____

    9. _____

    10. _____

Balaam and His Donkey
Review Page 3

2. List all of the titles and Scripture references studied so far.

    _____

    _____

    _____

    _____

    _____

    _____

    _____

    _____

    _____

    _____

    _____

    _____

    _____

Balaam and His Donkey
Review Page 4

2. (continued)

_____

_____

_____

_____

_____

_____

_____

_____

_____

_____

_____

_____

_____

_____

_____

_____

MOSES DIES; JOSHUA ASSUMES COMMAND
Worksheet

1. What is the date for Moses Dies; Joshua Assumes Command?

   _____

   _____

2. What is the Scripture reference for Moses Dies; Joshua Assumes Command?

   _____

   _____

3. Why did God not allow Moses to enter the Promised Land?

   _____

   _____

   _____

   _____

4. From what mountain could Moses view the Promised Land?

   _____

   _____

   _____

5. What happened to Moses' body after he died?

   _____

   _____

   _____

   _____

MOSES DIES; JOSHUA ASSUMES COMMAND
Worksheet, Page 2

6. Who became the new leader of the Israelites after Moses died?

_____

_____

_____

7. What does Joshua's name mean?

_____

_____

_____

8. Why did Moses stand with Joshua before all the people?

_____

_____

_____

_____

_____

MOSES DIES; JOSHUA ASSUMES COMMAND
Project 1—Bible Reading

Read Deuteronomy 34. Write a sentence using each of the words below, explaining its use in the story.

Mt. Nebo

_____

_____

cross over

_____

_____

buried

_____

_____

thirty

_____

_____

Joshua

_____

_____

face to face

_____

_____

Moses Dies; Joshua Assumes Command
Project 2

An obituary is a writing used in newspapers to let people know of the death of community members and pay a last tribute to that person. Write an obituary for Moses. Include how old he was (check your Bible), describe the event of his death, and briefly tell at least three things he did or stories about him. If you can, tell who was in his family and who will miss him (someone with whom he would have worked closely).

MOSES DIES; JOSHUA ASSUMES COMMAND
Test

1. What is the date for Moses Dies; Joshua Assumes Command?

    _____

    _____

2. What is the Scripture reference for Moses Dies; Joshua Assumes Command?

    _____

    _____

3. What was Moses' punishment for not believing God's Word?

    _____

    _____

    _____

    _____

4. What did Moses do on Mt. Nebo?

    _____

    _____

    _____

    _____

5. Who buried Moses?

    _____

    _____

    _____

6. What was Joshua chosen to do?

    _____

    _____

    _____

    _____

MOSES DIES; JOSHUA ASSUMES COMMAND
Test, Page 2

7. What does Joshua's name mean?

_____

_____

_____

8. How did the Israelites come to know that Joshua would be their new leader?

_____

_____

_____

_____

_____

Review

1. What modern day people are believed to be the descendants of Ishmael?

_____

_____

_____

2. What was to be done with firstborn animals?

_____

_____

_____

3. How long was Moses on Mt. Sinai when God made a second copy of the
   Ten Commandments?

_____

_____

_____

MOSES DIES; JOSHUA ASSUMES COMMAND
Test, Page 3

4. What was the place in the Tabernacle that was blocked off by a curtain and no one but the High Priest could enter?

_____

_____

_____

5. Which tribe was given the responsibility of taking care of the Tabernacle and later the Temple of God?

_____

_____

6. List all of the titles and Scripture references studied so far.

_____

_____

_____

_____

_____

_____

_____

_____

_____

_____

MOSES DIES; JOSHUA ASSUMES COMMAND
Test, Page 4

6. (continued)

_____

_____

_____

_____

_____

_____

_____

_____

_____

_____

_____

_____

_____

_____

_____

_____

SPIES TO CANAAN
Worksheet

1. What is the date for Spies to Canaan?

   _____

   _____

   _____

2. What is the Scripture reference for Spies to Canaan?

   _____

   _____

   _____

3. What city was the first target for the Hebrews in their conquest of the Promised Land?

   _____

   _____

4. Where did the Israelite spies find lodging and protection?

   _____

   _____

   _____

5. Why did the people of Jericho fear the Israelites and want to capture the Israelite spies?

   _____

   _____

   _____

   _____

SPIES TO CANAAN
Worksheet, Page 2

6. How did the Israelite spies escape from being captured?

_____

_____

_____

_____

7. How was Rahab blessed for her trust in God?

_____

_____

_____

8. Who is Rahab's famous son?

_____

_____

_____

_____

SPIES TO CANAAN
Project 1—Bible Reading

After reading the account of this story in the Bible you will know some specifics that were not included on the card.

Where did Rahab hide the spies?

_____

_____

_____

_____

_____

Which mighty act of God against the Egyptians caused Rahab's people to fear?

_____

_____

_____

_____

_____

What was Rahab to do in order to be spared?

_____

_____

_____

_____

_____

_____

SPIES TO CANAAN
Project 2—Thank You Note

The Hebrew spies sent into Jericho had much for which to be thankful. They particularly were indebted to Rahab. Assume you are one of the two spies that was sent to scout out Jericho. Write a thank-you letter to Rahab from the perspective of one of the spies. You may be creative when it comes to your name or details about yourself as the Bible gives no description about these men. But you must include at least five points from the story in your letter. Be sure to use the correct format for a friendly letter shown on the right.

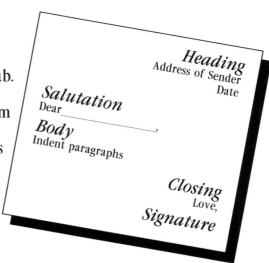

Heading
Address of Sender
Date

Salutation
Dear_____,

Body
Indent paragraphs

Closing
Love,

Signature

_____
_____
_____
_____
_____
_____
_____
_____
_____
_____
_____
_____
_____
_____
_____
_____

SPIES TO CANAAN
Test

1. What is the date for Spies to Canaan?

   _____

   _____

2. What is the Scripture reference for Spies to Canaan?

   _____

   _____

3. Why were the Israelite spies sent to Jericho?

   _____

   _____

   _____

   _____

4. Why were the people of Jericho trying to capture the spies?

   _____

   _____

   _____

   _____

5. What did Rahab do for the spies?

   _____

   _____

   _____

   _____

SPIES TO CANAAN
Test, Page 2

6. Describe Rahab.

_____

_____

_____

_____

_____

7. How did God bless Rahab?

_____

_____

_____

8. _____ is Rahab's son.

Review

1. What did the Israelites ask Aaron to make for them?

_____

_____

2. Name two things that were kept in the ark of the covenant.

_____

_____

_____

SPIES TO CANAAN
Test, Page 3

3. Who is the perfect High Priest who took the place of the Levites and Aaron's sons?

   _____

   _____

   _____

4. How many of the twelve spies thought that the Israelites could defeat the inhabitants of Canaan?

   _____

   _____

   _____

5. For how many years did the Israelites wander in the wilderness?

   _____

   _____

6. List all of the titles and Scripture references studied so far.

   _____

   _____

   _____

   _____

   _____

   _____

   _____

   _____

   _____

   _____

6. (continued)

_____

_____

_____

_____

_____

_____

_____

_____

_____

_____

_____

_____

_____

_____

_____

_____

_____

THE BATTLE OF JERICHO
Worksheet

1. What is the date for the Battle of Jericho?

   _____

   _____

2. What is the Scripture reference for the Battle of Jericho?

   _____

   _____

3. What did the commander of the army of heaven show Joshua?

   _____

   _____

   _____

4. What did the fighting men do for six days?

   _____

   _____

5. What did the fighting men do on the seventh day?

   _____

   _____

6. What happened to the walls of Jericho?

   _____

   _____

   _____

THE BATTLE OF JERICHO
Worksheet, Page 2

7. Who was spared from among the people of Jericho?

_____

_____

_____

8. How did the Israelites know which household was to be spared?

_____

_____

_____

_____

THE BATTLE OF JERICHO
Project 1—Bible Reading

Read about the Battle of Jericho in Joshua 5:13-6:27. Then number the following events in the order in which they occurred.

____ The Israelites and the ark marched around Jericho seven times

____ The people shouted

____ The Israelites marched around the city of Jericho once and returned to camp

____ The Israelite army rushed into the city and destroyed everything and everyone except Rahab

____ The Israelite army marched in silence once around the city for the next five days

____ The priests blew their trumpets

____ The commander of the army of the Lord met with Joshua

____ Jericho was burned

____ The walls of Jericho fell down

THE BATTLE OF JERICHO
Project 2

Write a newspaper article from the perspective of a citizen in Jericho. Your article in the Jericho Journal *should* describe what has been happening outside of your city.

Jericho Journal

_____

_____

_____

_____

_____

_____

_____

_____

_____

_____

_____

_____

_____

_____

_____

_____

_____

_____

THE BATTLE OF JERICHO
Test

1. What is the date for the Battle of Jericho?

   _____

   _____

2. What is the Scripture reference for the Battle of Jericho?

   _____

   _____

3. Whom did God send to meet with Joshua?

   _____

   _____

   _____

4. How many days did the Israelites march around the city?

   _____

   _____

   _____

5. What did the priests carry as they marched?

   _____

   _____

   _____

6. What did the Israelites do after they marched around the city on the last day?

   _____

   _____

   _____

   _____

THE BATTLE OF JERICHO
Test, Page 2

7. How did the Israelites get inside the city of Jericho?

_____

_____

_____

8. What did the Israelites do to the household that had a red ribbon in the window?

_____

_____

_____

Review

1. Because of his appreciation of Joseph, what did Pharaoh invite Joseph's family to do?

_____

_____

_____

2. Why did another pharaoh enslave the Israelites?

_____

_____

_____

_____

3. Describe the tabernacle.

_____

_____

_____

_____

_____

The Battle of Jericho
Test, Page 3

4. A priest is one who stands between _____

    and _____ .

5. What did the Moabites hire Balaam to do?

    _____

    _____

    _____

6. List all of the titles, Scripture references, and dates studied so far.

    _____

    _____

    _____

    _____

    _____

    _____

    _____

    _____

    _____

    _____

    _____

    _____

    _____

    _____

    _____

    _____

THE BATTLE OF JERICHO
Test, Page 4

6. (continued)

_____

_____

_____

_____

_____

_____

_____

_____

_____

_____

_____

_____

_____

_____

ISRAEL GIVEN THE PROMISED LAND
Worksheet

1. What is the date for Israel Given the Promised Land?

   _____

   _____

2. What is the Scripture reference for Israel Given the Promised Land?

   _____

   _____

3. Why were the Israelites able to conquer the Canaanites?

   _____

   _____

   _____

4. How were the Israelites disobedient to God's command?

   _____

   _____

   _____

5. What two things did the Israelites allow the Canaanites to do?

   _____

   _____

   _____

   _____

6. How did the Canaanites cause problems for many years after the conquest?

   _____

   _____

   _____

   _____

ISRAEL GIVEN THE PROMISED LAND
Worksheet, Page 2

7. Which tribe was the most faithful during the conquest?

_____

_____

_____

Israel Given the Promised Land
Project 1—Bible Reading

Read Joshua 21:43-45 and Judges 1:8-36. Then complete the crossword puzzle below.

Across

1. _____ gave Israel the Promised Land

3. God told Israel to _____ all of the Canaanites.

4. Some Israelites allowed their enemies to pay them _____.

6. Judah was not successful in the lowland because the people
living there used _____. (Judges 1:19)

Down

2. The land of _____ was the Promised Land.

3. Many of the Canaanites were allowed to _____ in the land.

4. The Israelites were _____ to follow the false gods of the Canaanites.

5. _____ was the only tribe that was obedient to God's command.

ISRAEL GIVEN PROMISED LAND
Project 2—Map

Pass out pages 2, 3 and 4. Have students study page 2 as you lead the discussion.

Discussion:

Which of 12 tribes did not have land? Why?
(Answer: Levi: they were to serve in the temple)

Do you see two names that are not part of the Twelve Tribes of Israel?
(Ephraim & Manasseh—Joseph's land was split and named for his two sons.)

Directions:

Reconstruct a map of Israel showing the portions occupied by each tribe. Photocopy the pieces on page 3 and then cut out the pieces on the copy. Use the map pictured to determine which tribe occupied each piece. There is one blank for each letter in the tribe name, so that should also help in determining which tribe goes with that piece. Color and decorate each piece. Using the picture on page 2 arrange the pieces to fit as they should inside the
border on page 4. Glue the pieces to the border page.

ISRAEL GIVEN PROMISED LAND
Project 2, Page 2

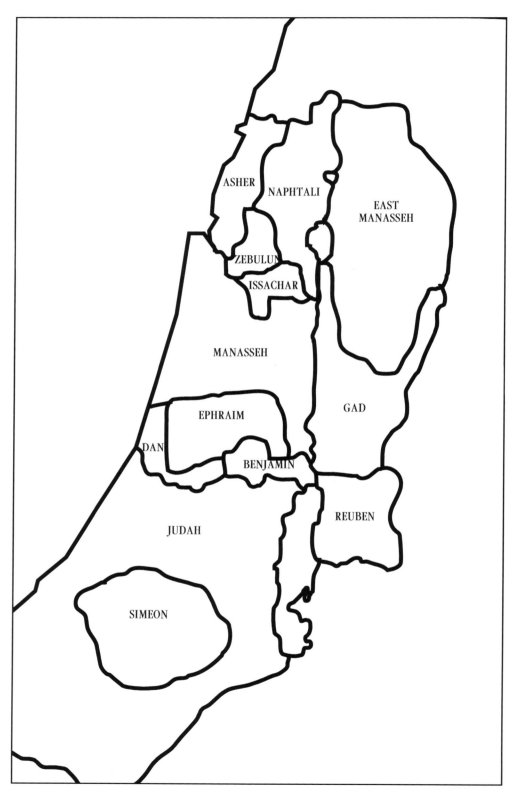

ISRAEL IS GIVEN THE PROMISED LAND
Project 2, Page 3

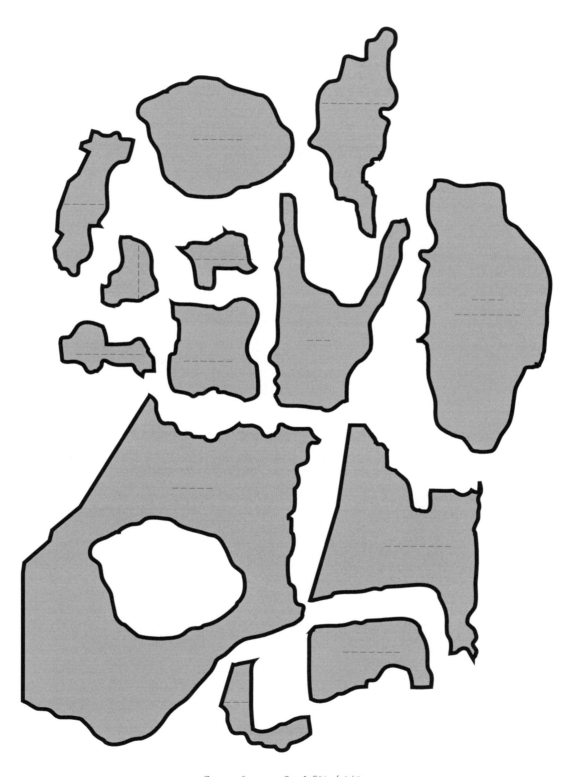

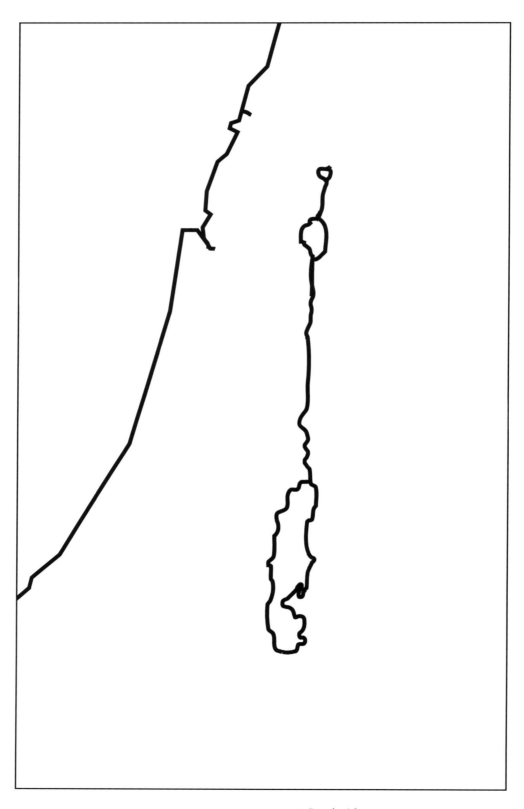

ISRAEL GIVEN THE PROMISED LAND
Project 3—Military Medals

Supplies

Ribbon (at least 1" wide)

construction paper

metallic finished paper

metallic colored spray paint

beads, sequins

safety pins

Directions

Medals can be made by taking a 5" long strip of ribbon and folding it in half. Students design the medallion part by using a variety of supplies provided by you (some are suggested here). Glue the medallion part to the two ends of ribbon. Concealing the head of the pin in between the folded ribbon, run the point through the back half of the ribbon.

Read this to the students:

You are the commander in chief of the Israelite army and you wish to commend one tribe for their superior following of their orders. Which tribe would that be? (Judah) What were those orders? (To take control of the land and drive out and destroy all Canaanites living there). You are going to design a medal for them using the supplies provided. You will also complete the presentation speech that would be read when the medal is given.

ISRAEL GIVEN THE PROMISED LAND
Test

1. What is the date for Israel Given the Promised Land?

   _____

   _____

2. What is the Scripture reference for Israel Given the Promised Land?

   _____

   _____

3. Who enabled the Israelites to conquer the Canaanites?

   _____

   _____

4. What had God commanded the Israelites to do to the Canaanites?

   _____

   _____

   _____

5. How did the Israelites disobey God's command?

   _____

   _____

   _____

   _____

6. What did the Canaanites tempt Israel to do?

   _____

   _____

   _____

   _____

ISRAEL GIVEN THE PROMISED LAND
Test, Page 2

7. Which tribe was the most faithful in obeying God's command?

_____

_____

_____

Review

1. What sign did God give Noah that he would not flood the earth again?

_____

_____

_____

2. What happened to Lot's wife?

_____

_____

_____

3. Who did Moses tell the Israelites would lead them after he died?

_____

_____

_____

4. Tell one thing about the death of Moses.

_____

_____

_____

_____

ISRAEL GIVEN THE PROMISED LAND
Test, Page 3

5. Who was the woman that hid the spies that Joshua sent into Jericho?

   _____

   _____

   _____

6. List all of the titles and Scripture references studied so far.

   _____

   _____

   _____

   _____

   _____

   _____

   _____

   _____

   _____

   _____

   _____

   _____

   _____

   _____

   _____

   _____

   _____

6. (continued)

_____

_____

_____

_____

_____

_____

_____

_____

_____

_____

_____

_____

_____

Joshua's Last Words
Worksheet

1. What is the date for Joshua's Last Words?

   _____

   _____

2. What is the Scripture reference for Joshua's Last Words?

   _____

   _____

3. Why did Joshua call all of the tribes of Israel to him before he died?

   _____

   _____

   _____

   _____

4. List three things that Joshua told the people before he died.

   a. _____

   b. _____

   c. _____

5. What did Joshua say would happen if the people worshipped other gods?

   _____

   _____

   _____

   _____

6. How did the people respond to Joshua's last words?

   _____

   _____

   _____

   _____

JOSHUA'S LAST WORDS
Project 1—Bible Reading

Read the following Biblical Passage from Joshua 23, 24:1-28 in the New King James Version. Use your knowledge from your previous study. Fill in the blanks. Then use your Bible to check your work and fill in the blanks of any you were unsure of.

Chapter 23

Now it came to pass, a long time after the LORD had given rest to Israel from all their enemies round about, that Joshua was old, advanced in age. And Joshua called for all Israel, for their elders, for their heads, for their judges, and for their officers, and said to them:

"I am old, advanced in age. You have seen all that the LORD your God has done to all these nations because of you, for the LORD your God is He who has _____ for you. See, I have divided to you by lot these nations that remain, to be an inheritance for your tribes, from the Jordan, with all the nations that I have cut off, as far as the Great Sea westward. And the LORD your God will expel them from before you and drive them out of your sight. So you shall possess their _____, as the LORD your God promised you.

Therefore be very courageous to keep and to do all that is written in the Book of the Law of Moses, lest you turn aside from it to the right hand or to the left, and lest you go among these nations, these who remain among you. You shall not make mention of the name of their gods, nor cause anyone to swear by them; you shall not serve them nor bow down to them, but you shall hold fast to the _____ your God, as you have done to this day.

For the LORD has driven out from before you great and strong nations; but as for you, no one has been able to stand against you to this day. One man of you shall chase a thousand, for the LORD your God is He who fights for you, as He promised you. Therefore take careful heed to yourselves, that you love the LORD your God. Or else, if indeed you do go back, and cling to the remnant of these nations—these that remain among you—and make _____ with them, and go in to them and they to you, know for certain that the LORD your God will no longer drive out these nations from before you. But they shall be snares and traps to you, and scourges on your sides and thorns in your eyes, until you perish from this good land which the LORD your God has given you.

"Behold, this day I am going the way of all the earth. And you know in all your _____ and in all your souls that not one thing has failed of all the good things which the LORD your God spoke concerning you. All have come to pass for you; not one word of them has failed. Therefore it shall come to pass, that as all the good things have come upon you which the LORD your God _____ you, so the LORD will bring upon you all harmful things, until He has destroyed you from this good land which the LORD your God has given you. When you have transgressed the _____ of the LORD your God, which He commanded you, and have gone and served other gods, and bowed down to them, then the _____ of the LORD will burn against you, and you shall perish quickly from the good land which He has given you."

Joshua's Last Words
Project 1—Bible Reading, Page 2

Chapter 24

Then Joshua gathered all the _____ of Israel to Shechem and called for the elders of Israel, for their heads, for their judges, and for their officers; and they presented themselves before God. And Joshua said to all the people, "Thus says the LORD God of Israel: 'Your fathers, including Terah, the father of Abraham and the father of Nahor, dwelt on the other side of the River in old times; and they served other gods. Then I took your father Abraham from the other side of the River, led him throughout all the land of _____, and multiplied his descendants and gave him Isaac. To Isaac I gave _____ and _____. To Esau I gave the mountains of Seir to possess, but Jacob and his children went down to Egypt. Also I sent _____ and Aaron, and I plagued Egypt, according to what I did among them. Afterward I brought you out.

'Then I brought your fathers out of Egypt, and you came to the sea; and the Egyptians pursued your fathers with _____ and horsemen to the ____ Sea. So they cried out to the LORD; and He put darkness between you and the Egyptians, brought the sea upon them, and covered them. And your eyes saw what I did in Egypt. Then you dwelt in the wilderness a long time. And I brought you into the land of the Amorites, who dwelt on the other side of the Jordan, and they fought with you. But I gave them into your hand, that you might possess their land, and I destroyed them from before you. Then Balak the son of Zippor, king of Moab, arose to make war against Israel, and sent and called Balaam the son of Beor to curse you. But I would not listen to Balaam; therefore he continued to _____ you. So I delivered you out of his hand. Then you went over the Jordan and came to Jericho. And the men of Jericho fought against you—also the Amorites, the Perizzites, the Canaanites, the Hittites, the Girgashites, the Hivites, and the Jebusites. But I delivered them into your hand. I sent the hornet before you which drove them out from before you, also the two kings of the Amorites, but not with your sword or with your bow. I have given you a land for which you did not labor, and cities which you did not build, and you dwell in them; you eat of the vineyards and olive groves which you did not _____.'

"Now therefore, fear the LORD, serve Him in sincerity and in truth, and put away the _____ which your

JOSHUA'S LAST WORDS
Project 1—Bible Reading, Page 3

fathers served on the other side of the River and in Egypt. Serve the LORD! And if it seems evil to you to serve the LORD, choose for yourselves this day whom you will serve, whether the gods which your fathers served that were on the other side of the River, or the gods of the Amorites, in whose land you dwell. But as for me and my house, we will serve the LORD."

So the people answered and said: "Far be it from us that we should forsake the LORD to serve other gods; for the LORD our God is He who brought us and our fathers up out of the land of _____, from the house of bondage, who did those great signs in our sight, and preserved us in all the way that we went and among all the people through whom we passed.

And the LORD drove out from before us all the people, including the Amorites who dwelt in the land. We also will serve the LORD, for He is our God."

But Joshua said to the people, "You cannot serve the LORD, for He is a holy God. He is a jealous God; He will not forgive your transgressions nor your sins. If you forsake the LORD and serve foreign _____, then He will turn and do you harm and consume you, after He has done you good."

And the people said to Joshua, "No, but we will serve the LORD!"

So Joshua said to the people, "You are witnesses against yourselves that you have chosen the LORD for yourselves, to serve Him." And they said, "We are witnesses!"

"Now therefore," he said, "put away the foreign gods which are among you, and incline your heart to the LORD God of Israel."

And the people said to Joshua, "The LORD our God we will serve, and His voice we will obey!"

So Joshua made a _____ with the people that day, and made for them a statute and an ordinance in Shechem. Then Joshua wrote these words in the Book of the Law of God. And he took a large stone, and set it up there under the oak that was by the sanctuary of the LORD. And Joshua said to all the people, "Behold, this stone shall be a witness to us, for it has heard all the words of the LORD which He spoke to us. It shall therefore be a witness to you, lest you deny your God." So Joshua let the people depart, each to his own inheritance.

And it came to pass after these things, that _____ the son of Nun, the servant of the LORD, died, being an hundred and ten years old. And they buried him in the border of his inheritance in Timnath-serah, which is in mount Ephraim, on the north side of the hill of Gaash. And Israel served the LORD all the days of Joshua, and all the days of the elders that outlived Joshua, and which had known all the works of the LORD, that he had done for Israel. And the bones of _____, which the children of Israel brought up out of Egypt, buried they in Shechem, in a parcel of ground which Jacob bought of the sons of Hamor the father of Shechem for an hundred pieces of silver: and it became the inheritance of the children of Joseph. And Eleazar the son of Aaron died; and they buried him in a hill that pertained to Phinehas his son, which was given him in mount Ephraim.

JOSHUA'S LAST WORDS
Project 2

Make a book containing the last things Joshua wanted to tell the people before he died. Each student will need three 5.5" x 8.5" pieces of paper. Put the three pieces together and fold them all in half so that you have a book of 6 5.5" x 4.25" pages. Staple through the fold so that the pages are bound together. The cover should be decorated with the title of the card, Scripture reference, and date. Glue the front cover to the next page so it is doubly thick and there are 8 pages inside the front and back covers. Cut out the word boxes and illustration boxes. Fit together the two word boxes that form each of the last things that Joshua said. Glue those word boxes on the left sides of each open page. Match the illustration boxes with the words that describe it. Glue the illustration boxes to the right sides of each open page across from the words that match the pictures.

He pleaded with them	*their history of God's great victories for them*
He reminded them	*to not forsake the Lord*
He warned them	*of God's blessing them with the Promised Land*
He recounted to them	*about what would happen if they broke the covenant*

JOSHUA'S LAST WORDS
Test

1. What is the date for Joshua's Last Words?

   _____

   _____

2. What is the Scripture reference for Joshua's Last Words?

   _____

   _____

3. What did Joshua do before he died?

   _____

   _____

   _____

   _____

4. List three things that Joshua told the people before he died.

   a. _____

   b. _____

   c. _____

5. What did Joshua say would happen if the people worshipped other gods?

   _____

   _____

   _____

   _____

6. Describe the reaction of the people to Joshua's last words.

   _____

   _____

   _____

   _____

JOSHUA'S LAST WORDS
Test, Page 2

Review

1. Name two things that the Israelites grumbled for when they left Egypt.

   _____

   _____

   _____

   _____

2. What miracle made Balaam aware that there was an angel blocking his path?

   _____

   _____

   _____

   _____

3. What did the Israelites do outside of Jericho for six days?

   _____

   _____

   _____

4. What did Rahab tie to her window so that she might be spared?

   _____

   _____

   _____

5. Which tribe was the most faithful at driving out and destroying the Canaanites in the Promised Land?

   _____

   _____

   _____

Joshua's Last Words
Test, Page 3

6. List all of the titles and Scripture references studied so far.

_____

_____

_____

_____

_____

_____

_____

_____

_____

_____

_____

_____

_____

_____

_____

_____

_____

_____

_____

6. (continued)

_____

_____

_____

_____

_____

_____

_____

_____

_____

_____

_____

MEMORY VERSES

The following is a listing of some suggested verses for memorization along with the card with which each would correspond. This list is purely supplemental and should be included as the teacher sees fit. The program contains enough without additional memory verses for most learning situations.

CREATION
Genesis 1:1/Genesis 1:27, 28

THE FALL
Genesis 3:15

GOD'S COVENANT WITH NOAH
Genesis 9:11

GOD'S COVENANT WITH ABRAHAM
Genesis 17:6, 7

FAMINE IN EGYPT
Genesis 45:5, 7, 8

PLAGUES IN EGYPT
Exodus 3:14

SPIES TO CANAAN
Numbers 14:8, 9

JOSHUA'S LAST WORDS
Joshua 24:15

ANY CARD
Deuteronomy 7:6-8/Deuteronomy 6:4

EPHOD→
EX. 28

BLUE ROBE→

WHITE→

THE HIGH PRIEST
IN ROBES OF GLORY AND BEAUTY

GENESIS THROUGH JOSHUA
Song Lyrics

The Bible chronologically through this song you'll know
Come now sing along with me learn from time ago
In Genesis chapters one and two God created all
Did it only in six days and then there came the fall
In Genesis chapter three the devil tempted Adam and Eve
To eat from the tree of wrong and right which wasn't right you see
In chapter four of Genesis the first kids on the block
Cain gave from his own garden and Abel gave from his own flock
God was pleased with Abel now Cain felt jealousy
Murdered his own brother then God cursed wicked Cain you see.
Enoch and Methuselah in Genesis chapter five
Lived to be the oldest man that had ever been alive
It's so very easy to memorize truth
Found in the history of God's holy book
Now, wickedness infiltrated the hearts of all mankind
So God sent the Flood to destroy them in Genesis six through nine
But Noah he found favor and built an ark so strong
That kept them safe for forty days so they could sail along
And when the floods receded in Genesis chapter nine
God made a covenant with Noah and put a rainbow in the sky
Then man became more foolish than he had ever been
And tried to build a tower called Babel in chapter eleven
In the year 2091 and Genesis twelve and thirteen
Abram was told to leave his home to make him a great nation
God makes a covenant with Abram in 2082 B.C.
Changed his name in chapter 15 through chapter 17
Its so very easy to memorize truth
Found in the history of God's holy book
Now Sarah she was barren had no children of her own
So Sarah's handmaiden Hagar had Ishmael Abram's son
This happened in Genesis sixteen and Genesis twenty-one
Back in 2080 B.C. and still there's more to come
Somewhere in between the story we just told
A city called Sodom and Gomorrah burned to the ground you know
God destroyed that city and rescued righteous Lot
In Genesis eighteen through nineteen but turned his wife into a pillar of salt
Somewhere in 2066 Abraham had a son
Then he named him Isaac in Genesis twenty-one
Then God told Abraham to make a sacrifice
And just before he did Isaac in a ram did God provide
It's so very easy to memorize truth
Found in the history of God's holy book

GENESIS THROUGH JOSHUA
Song Lyrics, Page 2

Now in Genesis twenty-four Abraham he goes to Ur
To seek out a wife for his son Isaac
And in 2026 his cousin he does pick
Rebekah a beautiful lady
Then in 2000 B.C. Rebekah she conceives
And has a pair of twins Jacob and Esau
And in Genesis twenty-five well Jacob tells a lie
To steal from his brother his blessing!
Now in 1898 Joseph became a slave
Because his other brothers didn't like him
And from Genesis thirty-seven through Genesis chapter forty
We see the life he lives way down in Egypt
Now a famine came to pass just like Pharaoh's dream at last
And started in 1878
And it lasted for seven years and caused a lot of fears
But through Joseph God gave them the answer
Now through Genesis twenty-nine and Genesis thirty-six
As well as forty-six through chapter fifty
Twelve Tribes of Israel the Jews their name as well
Descendants of Abraham in 1860
We're finally in a new book of the Bible
This wonderful history certainly comes alive
We're in the second book the one called Exodus
There's more song to be sung so sing with me
Now Moses was born in Egypt around 1525
Exodus one and two they tell about his early life
When Moses he got older God spoke through the burning bush
Go deliver my people Israel from the land of Egypt's curse
And so in 1446 God sent ten plagues on Egypt
In Exodus three through twelve you'll see Pharaoh finally give up
Shortly after Passover in that same old year
In chapters thirteen through fifteen the Exodus does appear
Ten Commandments were given in 1445
Written in chapters nineteen and twenty in them they should abide
Then Aaron did a foolish thing in 1444
He made a golden calf in chapter thirty-two and worshipped God no more
It's so very easy to memorize truth
Found in the history of God's holy book
Now after a great scolding in chapter thirty-four
Moses gets two new tablets of the law in 1444

Genesis through Joshua
Song Lyrics, Page 3

The Tabernacle and Ark of that old Covenant
Was described in Exodus thirty-six through chapter thirty-seven
All of this was given to show the sacrifice
In the years of 1444 through 1435
Now on to Numbers three the Levitical Priesthood starts
In 1440 B.C. to tend the Tabernacle and the Ark
The Wanderings in the Wilderness happen in Numbers nine
Through 1446 and fourteen hundred six in time
In Numbers 22, 23, 24 A story you cannot miss
A donkey spoke to Balaam in fourteen hundred six
It's so very easy to memorize truth
Found in the history of God's holy book
Deuteronomy thirty-four yes we still have a little more
Moses dies and Joshua takes command
And in fourteen hundred six because Moses disobeyed
Joshua leads the Jews into the Promised Land
Soon he sends the spies into Canaan
This is all found in his book chapter two
To spy on Jericho and Rahab hid the spies you know
So they spared her life when Israel came to conquer
We're almost at the end Israel's given the Promise land
Between 1400 and 1350 B.C.
In Joshua twenty-one and Judges chapter one
We see the wars of their entire history
And in Joshua twenty-three and twenty-four
Joshua stands to give his final word
And in thirteen hundred and ninety He reminds them finally
To follow the Lord forever!

ANSWERS

CREATION

Worksheet
1. Genesis 1, 2
2. No
3. God
4. Six
5. Day 1: day and night
   Day 2: heaven and earth
   Day 3: seas and land
   Day 4: sun, moon, and stars
   Day 5: creatures of the sky and sea
   Day 6: creatures of dry land and man
   Day 7: God rested.

Project 1
1. God told the creatures to multiply and fill the earth.
2. God saw that everything was good.
3. Darkness was on the face of the deep.
4. God made man in his own image.
5. God said, "Let there be light."
6. God told man to have dominion over the earth.
7. The firmament divided the waters above from the waters below.

Test
1. Genesis 1, 2
2. God
3. Day 1: day and night
   Day 2: heaven and earth
   Day 3: seas and land
   Day 4: sun, moon, and stars
   Day 5: creatures of the sky and sea
   Day 6: creatures of dry land and man
   Day 7: God rested.

THE FALL

Worksheet
1. Genesis 3
2. As a serpent
3. Eat of the Tree of Knowledge
4. He ate it.
5. If they ate of it they would die.
6. The world, everything
7. Man was now guilty before God.

Project 1
1. serpent
2. fruit
3. fig leaves
4. hid
5. belly
6. pain
7. toil, thorns, thistles
8. tunics
9. cherubim

Test
1. Genesis 3
2. Satan
3. Eat of the Tree of Knowledge
4. He ate it.
5. Eat of the Tree of Knowledge
6. It was cursed.
7. All man is now guilty before God.

CAIN AND ABEL

Worksheet
1. Genesis 4
2. Cain
3. Farmer
4. Shepherd
5. Fruit
6. The firstborn of his flock
7. Abel's offering
8. Cain

Project 1
1. Eve
2. God
3. God
4. Cain
5. Cain
6. God

ANSWERS

Test
1. Genesis 4
2. Adam and Eve
3. Farmer
4. The firstborn of his flock
5. Abel's offering
6. Cain murdered Abel.
7. He was unable to grow crops, and he became a wanderer.

ENOCH AND METHUSELAH
Worksheet
1. Genesis 5:21-32
2. Seth
3. Enoch's life was characterized by consistent faithfulness and righteousness.
4. He did not let him see death.
5. Enoch is the seventh generation after Adam in Seth's godly line.
6. Completeness
7. Methuselah was Enoch's son.
8. He lived longer than any other person that the Bible speaks of.
9. Methuselah was the grandfather of Noah.

Project 1
Methusalah dies
Enoch dies
Methuselah born
Challenge: 669 years
300 years

Project 2
930
912
905
910
895
962
365
969
Methusalah
Jared
Adam
Seth
Kenan
Enosh
Mahalel
Enoch

Test
1. Genesis 5:21-32
2. Seth
3. Enoch's life was characterized by consistent faithfulness and righteousness.
4. God did not let him see death.
5. Completeness
6. He lived longer than any other person that the Bible speaks of.
7. Methuselah was Enoch's son.
8. Methuselah was Noah's grandfather.

Review
1. Day 1: day and night
   Day 2: heaven and earth
   Day 3: seas and land
   Day 4: sun, moon, and stars
   Day 5: creatures of the sky and sea
   Day 6: creatures of dry land and man
2. They would die.
3. Satan
4. Shepherd
5. See the master list on page 282.

THE FLOOD
Worksheet
1. Genesis 6-9
2. His every intent was wicked.
3. Noah
4. Male and female of every species along with his family
5. Forty days and nights
6. They were destroyed.
7. That he would never flood the earth again
8. The rainbow

Project 1

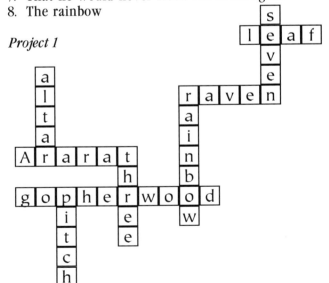

Answers

Test
1. Genesis 6-9
2. God observed that man was wicked, so he said he would destroy man.
3. Noah found grace in the eyes of the Lord.
4. Build an ark
5. Put them in the ark
6. It rained.
7. Never destroy the earth with a flood again
8. The rainbow

Review
1. His work became difficult.
2. Jesus
3. Fruit
4. Cain murdered Abel
5. He lived longer than any other person that the Bible speaks of.

God's Covenant with Noah

Worksheet
1. Genesis 9:1-17
2. A covenant is like a promise.
3. Noah and God
4. He would never again destroy the earth with a flood.
5. The rainbow
6. It reminded Noah of God's promise to never again destroy the earth with a flood.

Project 1
The basket should be filled with fruits, grains and vegetables ("every herb that yields seed and every tree whose fruit yields seed"). On the right should be fruits, grains, vegetables ("every herb that yields seed and every tree whose fruit yields seed") and animals ("every moving thing that lives"). And there should be a rainbow in the sky.

Project 2
God/Noah/that he would never again destroy the earth with a flood/rainbow

Answers will vary.

Test
1. Genesis 9:1-17
2. A covenant is like a promise.
3. Noah and God participated in the first covenant that is described in the Bible.
4. He would never again destroy the earth with a flood.
5. The promise was for Noah and his descendants.
6. The rainbow
7. It should remind you of God's promise to never again destroy the earth with a flood.

Review
1. No
2. She would become like God.
3. Adam and Eve
4. Abel
5. He did not see death.
6. See the master list on page 282.

The Tower of Babel

Worksheet
1. Genesis 11
2. One
3. Of their accomplishments
4. He caused them to speak different languages, and he scattered them abroad.
5. The ziggurat of Marduk at Babylon

Project 1
1. language
2. bricks, asphalt
3. city, tower, heavens
4. confused, scattered
5. Babel

Project 2
God saw their pride (3rd)
God scattered the people (4th)
Everyone spoke one language (1st)
They built a high tower (2nd)
Answers will vary
Answers will vary

Project 3
1. Stairs begin and end nowhere, windows opening into walls, half is being built while half is in ruin, etc.
2. He is absorbed in the homage he is receiving instead of seeing the hard work the stone masons are doing or the ridiculous state the tower is in
3. The Roman Colosseum

ANSWERS

Test
1. Genesis 11
2. one
3. tower
4. the people's pride
5. many languages/scatter
6. it is the Tower of Babel

Review
1. Eve
2. animals
3. Cain
4. Enoch
5. Noah
6. See the master list on page 282.

THE CALL OF ABRAM
Worksheet
1. c. 2091 B.C.
2. Genesis 12, 13
3. Ur, Mesopotamia
4. Sarai
5. Lot and Sarai
6. Canaan
7. God told him he would give the land to Abram's descendants.

Project 1

Project 2
He lived in a tent.
He had only a few family members for company.
He worshipped God.
He had fewer possessions.
He had to grow or make everything himself.
He did not know where God was taking him.

Test
1. c. 2091 B.C.
2. Genesis 12, 13
3. Ur, Mesopotamia
4. Abram's wife
5. Abram's nephew
6. No
7. Canaan

Review
1. Rested
2. Adam and Eve
3. Noah
4. With a flood
5. A promise
6. That he would never again destroy the earth with a flood
7. See the master list on page 282.

GOD'S COVENANT WITH ABRAHAM
Worksheet
1. c. 2082 B.C.
2. Genesis 15–17
3. He would make him a great nation.
4. Children
5. Heifer, goat, ram
6. A smoking oven and a burning torch
7. Circumcision

Project 1
1. Descendants, stars
2. Land

1. Heifer, goat, ram
2. Vultures
3. 400, possessions, land
4. Smoking oven, burning torch

1. Circumcised

1. Abraham
2. Sarah

ANSWERS

Project 2
1. God told Abraham that his descendants would outnumber the stars.
2. Abraham cut animals in two pieces
3. A smoking oven and a burning torch passed between the pieces of the animals.

Test
1. c. 2082 B.C.
2. Genesis 15–17
3. He would make him a great nation.
4. Children
5. He cut them in two pieces.
6. He passed between the pieces of the animals.
7. No

Review
1. Six
2. She would have pain in childbirth.
3. Seth
4. In an ark
5. One
6. Abram's wife
7. See the master list on page 282.

HAGAR AND ISHMAEL
Worksheet
1. c. 2080 B.C.
2. Genesis 16, 21
3. A child
4. To produce a child

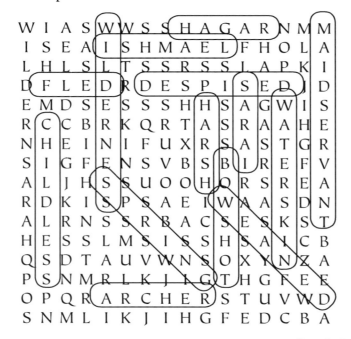

5. Harshly
6. They would be many.
7. Cast Hagar and Ishmael out into the wilderness
8. Arabs

Project 2
Sarah:
  Isaac
  treated the other harshly
  Sarai
  90
Hagar:
  maidservant
  Ishmael
  Arabs
  ran away
  scoffed at a feast of weaning
  visited by an angel

Test
1. c. 2080 B.C.
2. Genesis 16, 21
3. Sarah's
4. To produce a child
5. Ishmael
6. God would multiply them.
7. Abraham cast her and Ishmael out into the wilderness
8. Arabs

Review
1. He was jealous because God accepted Abel's offering and not his.
2. Male and female of every species
3. The rainbow
4. The ziggurat of Marduk at Babylon
5. He confused their language and scattered them abroad.
6. Lot
7. See the master list on page 282.

SODOM AND GOMORRAH
Worksheet
1. c. 2080 B.C.
2. Genesis 18, 19
3. Destroy it
4. Spared the cities
5. Lot
6. She looked back.
7. She was turned into a pillar of salt.
8. Keep the way of the Lord, do righteousness and justice

ANSWERS

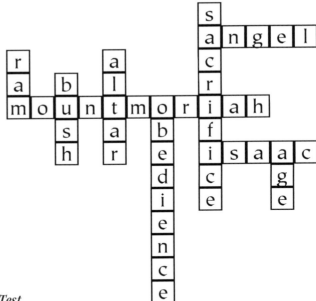

Project 1
1. They put their hands out of the door and pulled Lot inside. Then they made the wicked men blind so that they could not find the door.
2. He went to live in a cave in the mountains.
3. His two unmarried daughters

Test
1. c. 2080 B.C.
2. Genesis 18, 19
3. Abraham
4. Ten righteous men
5. He was the only righteous man and was rescued from the city.
6. She looked back.
7. She was turned into a pillar of salt.
8. Keep the way of the Lord, do righteousness and justice

Review
1. Death entered the world, and all men are guilty before God.
2. Enoch
3. An ark
4. They were sinfully proud of their tower.
5. He would make him a great nation.
6. Abraham and Hagar
7. See the master list on page 282.

BIRTH AND SACRIFICE OF ISAAC
Worksheet
1. c. 2066 B.C.
2. Genesis 21, 22
3. Abraham was 100 and Sarah was 91.
4. Sacrifice him
5. Mount Moriah
6. An angel of the Lord
7. A ram caught in the nearby bushes
8. His faithfulness and obedience

Project 1
2/8/9/1/4/10/5/3/6/11/7

Test
1. c. 2066 B.C.
2. Genesis 21, 22
3. Abraham was 100 and Sarah was 91.
4. To sacrifice him
5. An altar
6. An angel of the Lord
7. A ram
8. God was pleased with the faith and obedience of Abraham.

Review
1. He had Noah build an ark and live in it with all of the animals while God flooded the earth.
2. Canaan
3. Abraham, two, smoking oven and burning torch
4. Hagar
5. 91
6. See the master list on page 282.

ISAAC AND REBEKAH
Worksheet
1. c. 2026 B.C.
2. Genesis 24
3. A trusted servant
4. She would offer to water his camels.
5. Rebekah
6. The girl was Isaac's cousin.
7. The next day

ANSWERS

Project 1
1. Under the thigh
2. Golden nose ring and two bracelets
3. Until he told about his errand
4. Ten
5. Rebekah

Test
1. c. 2026 B.C.
2. Genesis 24
3. Find a wife for Isaac
4. Rebekah
5. She offered to water his camels.
6. The girl was Isaac's cousin.
7. Rebekah left her home the next day to go with the servant and marry Isaac.

Review
1. Day 1: Day and night
   Day 2: heaven and earth
   Day 3: seas and land
   Day 4: sun, moon, and stars
   Day 5: creatures of the sky and sea
   Day 6: creatures of dry land and man
   Day 7: God rested.
2. Cain
3. A promise
4. A tower
5. Sarah
6. Spared the cities
7. See the master list on page 282.

JACOB AND ESAU
Worksheet
1. c. 2000 B.C.
2. Genesis 25:19–34; 27:1–46
3. The older would serve the younger.
4. The firstborn was named Esau.
5. The name Jacob means "grabber."
6. It entitles the oldest son to the largest share of his father's estate.
7. A pot of soup
8. Isaac was old and blind.
9. Give Esau his blessing
10. He felt his hands and neck.
11. He put goat hair on his hands and neck.

Project 1
1. heel: When Jacob was born he was grabbing the heel of Esau.

lentils: Esau sold his birthright for Jacob's stew of lentils.

smooth-skinned: Jacob wore goat skins on his neck and hands because he was smooth-skinned.

blind: Isaac was basically blind so he could not tell that he was blessing Jacob instead of Esau.
2. Kill Jacob
3. Rebekah
4. His uncle Laban's place

Test
1. c. 2000 B.C.
2. Genesis 25:19–34; 27:1–46
3. Answers will vary. See card.

Review
1. Eat of the Tree of Knowledge
2. Completeness
3. The rainbow
4. Answers will vary.
5. Harshly
6. Mt. Moriah
7. See the master list on page 282.

JOSEPH AS A SLAVE
Worksheet
1. c. 1898 B.C.
2. Genesis 37–40
3. He dreamt that his brothers and parents would bow down to him as ruler.
4. For his dreams and the coat his father gave him
5. Kill him
6. Reuben
7. Midianite traders
8. It was smeared with animal blood.
9. He was falsely accused by Potiphar's wife.

Project 1
BUTLER
Picture: A vine with 3 branches of grapes was pressed into wine for Pharaoh's cup. The butler gave Pharaoh the cup.
Writing: In three days the butler will get his old job back.
BAKER
Picture: Three baskets filled with baked goods. Birds ate out of the top basket which was on his head.
Writing: In three days Pharaoh will hang him and birds will eat his flesh.

ANSWERS

Project 2
Joseph being sold into slavery to the Egyptians
slavery
Egypt
His brothers sold him
They were jealous
his brother

Joseph in prison
prison
Egypt
he was falsely accused
He rejected the advances of a woman
Potipher's wife

Test
1. c. 1898 B.C.
2. Genesis 37–40
3. He dreamt that his brothers and parents would bow down to him as ruler.
4. Kill him
5. He convinced his brothers to put him into a pit alive.
6. His brothers sold him to Midianite traders.
7. Egypt
8. The brothers had smeared his coat with animal's blood.
9. Potiphar's wife

Review
1. They were evil.
2. Ur, Mesopotamia
3. Answers will vary.
4. Ishmael
5. Lot
6. A ram
7. See the master list on page 282.

FAMINE IN EGYPT
Worksheet
1. c. 1878–1871 B.C.
2. Genesis 41–47
3. The butler
4. God
5. There would be seven years of famine after seven years of plenty.
6. Second-in-command
7. Joseph's brothers
8. Come live in Goshen

Project
1. Seven years of famine
2. Signet ring, garments of fine linen, gold chain
3. Spies
4. Benjamin
5. A silver cup

Test
1. c. 1878–1871 B.C.
2. Genesis 41–47
3. He told Pharaoh of Joseph's ability to interpret dreams.
4. Pharaoh's dreams indicated that there would be seven years of plenty before seven years of famine.
5. He made him second-in-command.
6. Storehouses
7. To buy grain
8. No
9. Joseph's family

Review
1. Answers will vary.
2. He confused their language and caused them to scatter abroad.
3. Circumcision
4. An angel of the Lord
5. 100
6. She offered to water his camels for him.
7. See the master list on page 282.

TWELVE TRIBES OF ISRAEL
Worksheet
1. c. 1860 B.C.
2. Genesis 29–36, 46–50
3. A great nation would come from his descendants.
4. Abraham, Isaac, and Jacob
5. Israel
6. Twelve
7. The twelve tribes of Israel

Project 2
Row 1: Simeon, Naphtali, Issachar; Row 2: Benjamin, Ephraim, Gad; Row 3: Judah, Manasseh, Zebulun; Row 4: Dan, Reuben, Asher

Project 3
1. Give her honor, to reflect how much he loved his wife, etc.
2. Joseph is second-in-command and Asenath is his wife
3. Rembrandt's time period

ANSWERS

4. So the viewer would identify personally with the event
5. Jacob tricking his father to receive Esau's blessing
6. Jacob's hands—to show the importance of the event

Test
1. c. 1860 B.C.
2. Genesis 29-36, 46-50
3. A great nation would come from his descendants.
4. The patriarchs
5. God changed Jacob's name to Israel.
6. Jacob had twelve sons and they became the Israelites.
7. The twelve tribes of Israel

Review
1. As a serpent
2. Enoch
3. Noah
4. She looked back at Sodom and Gomorrah.
5. Rebekah
6. Some soup
7. See the master list on page 282.

MOSES' BIRTH
Worksheet
1. c. 1525 B.C.
2. Exodus 1,2
3. They were numerous.
4. He enslaved them.

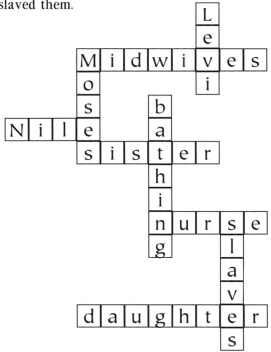

5. Kill all Israelite baby boys when they were born.
6. They hid him and then put him in a basket on the Nile River.
7. Pharaoh's daughter
8. To draw out

Project 2
Egypt
My people were enslaved and all the baby boys were being killed
Israelite
Levi
to hide me because I was beautiful
Moses, draw out
in an ark on the river Nile
the palace of Pharaoh
wealth & luxury (answers may vary, be creative)

Test
1. c. 1525 B.C.
2. Exodus 1, 2
3. He feared how numerous they were becoming.
4. The Hebrew midwives were ordered by Pharaoh to kill all Israelite baby boys when they were born. They feared God so they did not obey Pharaoh.
5. Levi
6. He was put in a basket on the Nile River.
7. Pharaoh's daughter
8. Moses' older sister
9. Moses' mother

Review
1. Male and female of every species
2. He would make him a great nation.
3. To produce a child
4. They were cousins.
5. He covered himself with goat hair.
6. They smeared his coat with animal blood.
7. See the master list on page 282.

PLAGUES IN EGYPT
Worksheet
1. c. 1446 B.C.
2. Exodus 3–12
3. A burning bush
4. Free them from slavery
5. Aaron
6. That they be allowed to go into the wilderness to worship God
7. A plague
8. An Egyptian god

ANSWERS

Project
See description of the event on the card. Answers will vary.

Test
1. c. 1446 B.C.
2. Exodus 3-12
3. God spoke to Moses through a burning bush and called him to free the Israelites from Egyptian slavery.
4. To allow them to go into the wilderness to worship God
5. Aaron
6. Ten
7. Each time Pharaoh refused God sent a plague which was a direct attack on a false Egyptian god.

Review
1. Methuselah
2. They were past the childbearing years.
3. Jacob and Esau
4. Because of his dreams and the coat their father gave him
5. Potiphar
6. There would be seven years of plenty followed by seven years of famine.
7. See the master list on page 282.

THE EXODUS
Worksheet
1. c. 1446 B.C.
2. Exodus 13-15
3. All firstborn of families and animals were killed.
4. Putting lamb's blood on their doorposts
5. Passover
6. By the Red Sea
7. He tried to recapture the Israelites to enslave them again.
8. God parted the Red Sea so that the Israelites could walk through. When the Egyptians tried to follow them, God let the waters go back, killing them.

Project 1
After Pharaoh let the Israelites go, then he changed his mind and pursued the Israelites.
The Israelites were camping by the sea when Pharaoh's army caught up with them.
Moses stretched out his hands and the waters parted.
A pillar of cloud came between the Israelites and the Egyptians.
The waters went back and the chariots and horsemen of the Pharaohs drowned.

Test
1. c. 1446 B.C.
2. Exodus 13-15
3. Ten
4. God killed the firstborn of all families and animals.
5. Lamb's blood
6. The Red Sea
7. God parted the Red Sea so that the Israelites could walk through.
8. They were drowned.

Review
1. He was grabbing his twin brother's heel when he was born.
2. Abraham, Isaac, Jacob, Joseph
3. Famine
4. See the master list on page 282.

THE TEN COMMANDMENTS
Worksheet
1. c. 1445 B.C.
2. Exodus 19, 20
3. The Ten Commandments
4. Stone tablets
5. 1. You shall have no other gods before me. 2. You shall not make for yourself a carved image. 3. You shall not take the name of the Lord your God in vain. 4. Remember the Sabbath day to keep it holy. 5. Honor your father and mother. 6. You shall not murder. 7. You shall not commit adultery. 8. You shall not steal. 9. You shall not bear false witness against your neighbor. 10. You shall not covet.

Project 1
1. Clothes
2. Bounds, touch
3. Cloud
4. Smoke, fire, quaked

ANSWERS

Project 2
Each row of the chart is in order below. What is Required has an "r" next to the commandment number, and What is Forbidden has an "f".

1 You shall have no other gods before me.
1r to know and acknowledge God to be the only true God
1f the denying, or not worshipping and glorifying
2 You shall not make for yourself a carved image.
2r the receiving, observing, and keeping pure
2f the worshipping of God by images
3 You shall not take the name of the Lord your God in vain.
3r the holy and reverent use of all God's names
3f profaning or abusing of anything
4 Remember the Sabbath day, to keep it holy.
4r a holy resting all that day
4f the omission, or careless performance
5 Honor your father and mother.
5r preserving the honor, and performing
5f the neglecting of or doing anything against
6 You shall not murder.
6r all lawful endeavors to preserve
6f the taking away of our own life
7 You shall not commit adultery.
7r the preservation of our own
7f all unchaste thoughts, words
8 You shall not steal.
8r the lawful procuring and furthering
8f whatsoever doth, or may, unjustly hinder
9 You shall not bear false witness against your neighbor.
9r the maintaining and promoting of truth
9f whatsoever is prejudicial to truth,
10 You shall not covet.
10r full contentment with our own condition
10f all discontentment with our own estate

Test
1. c. 1445 B.C.
2. Exodus 19, 20
3. Mt. Sinai
4. God
5. 1. You shall have no other gods before me.
2. You shall not make for yourself a carved image. 3. You shall not take the name of the Lord your God in vain. 4. Remember the Sabbath day to keep it holy. 5. Honor your father and mother. 6. You shall not murder. 7. You shall not commit

adultery. 8. You shall not steal. 9. You shall not bear false witness against your neighbor. 10. You shall not covet.

Review
1. Abram
2. Sacrifice him
3. His servant
4. 12
5. Kill all of the Hebrew boys when they were born
6. See the master list on page 282.

AARON AND THE GOLDEN CALF
Worksheet
1. c. 1444 B.C.
2. Exodus 32
3. Make a golden calf
4. Destroy the Israelites
5. Threw down the stone tablets and broke them
6. The covenant was broken.
7. He reminded God of the promises he made and turned away God's wrath.
8. He stood between God and his people.

Project 1
They didn't know, maybe died.
Earrings
burned offerings, drink, play
war

Moses threw down threw down the stone tablets and they broke at the foot of the mountain. He burned the golden calf and ground it into powder. Then he scattered it in the water so that the Israelites had to drink it. Many people were put to death, and God plagued the people.

Test
1. c. 1444 B.C.
2. Exodus 32
3. They wanted a god they could see and carry before them.
4. Make a golden calf
5. He threw down the stone tablets and broke them.
6. The covenant was broken.
7. Jesus

ANSWERS

Review
1. Cain and Abel; Esau and Jacob
2. An angel of the Lord
3. Potiphar's wife falsely accused him.
4. He interpreted Pharaoh's dream.
5. See the master list on page 282.

MOSES GETS NEW TABLETS
Worksheet
1. c. 1444 B.C.
2. Exodus 34
3. Two more stone tablets
4. The Israelites were described as stiff-necked like the cow they worshiped.
5. Make a covenant with the people that God was going to destroy before them
6. They were to be sacrificed.
7. 40 days
8. His face shone brightly.
9. A veil

Project 1
forty
sabbath
tablets
bread
stiff-necked
Sinai
veil
firstborn
shining

Test
1. c. 1444 B.C.
2. Exodus 34
3. The Law—the Ten Commandments
4. Mt. Sinai
5. The people that God was going to destroy before them
6. Sacrifice them
7. It lasted 40 days. He had no food.
8. His face shone brightly.
9. A veil

Review
1. Cain
2. God would multiply them.
3. Reuben, Simeon, Levi, Judah, Issachar, Zebulun, Joseph, Benjamin, Gad, Asher, Dan, Naphtali
4. He was placed in a basket to float on the Nile River.
5. See the master list on page 282.

THE TABERNACLE AND THE ARK OF THE COVENANT
Worksheet
1. c. 1444–1435 B.C.
2. Exodus 36–37
3. Bezaleel and Aholiab
4. Tell them to stop giving
5. A holy place where the priests met with God, a tent lined with beautiful fabrics and furs
6. Golden candle stand, table of show bread, a curtain to block off the Most Holy Place
7. Wooden box overlaid with gold
8. Go into the Most Holy Place and sprinkle lamb's blood on the ark
9. The things kept in the ark of the covenant all reminded the people of God's faithfulness.

Project 1
Colors - scarlet, blue, purple
Metals - gold, bronze, silver
Fabrics & Furs - ram skins, badger skins, goat hair, linen, thread
Decorations - almond blossoms, flowers

Test
1. c. 1444–1435 B.C.
2. Exodus 36–37
3. Bezaleel and Aholiab were two of the main craftsmen that worked on the tabernacle.
4. Golden candle stand, table of show bread, a curtain to block off the Most Holy Place
5. The curtain in the tabernacle blocked people off from the Most Holy Place.
6. The ark of the covenant
7. Wooden box overlaid with gold
8. Went into the Most Holy Place and sprinkled lamb's blood on the ark
9. That God forgave their sins only when blood was shed
10. The Ten Commandments, Aaron's staff, jar of manna

ANSWERS

Review
1. Noah, Abraham
2. In a pit
3. Pharaoh's daughter
4. Aaron
5. Lamb's blood
6. See the master list on page 282.

THE LEVITICAL PRIESTHOOD BEGINS
Worksheet
1. c. 1440 B.C.
2. Numbers 3
3. Levites
4. Give an offering
5. The Lord was to be their inheritance.
6. One who stands between God and the people
7. Jesus

Test
1. c. 1440 B.C.
2. Numbers 3
3. Levites were to carry the tabernacle and help the sons of Aaron.
4. There were more firstborn than Levites.
5. Land
6. A priest is one who stands between God and the people.
7. Jesus is our High Priest.

Review
1. Sacrifice his son
2. It is the right of the oldest son to inherit the largest portion of his father's estate.
3. Ten
4. Passover
5. Mt. Sinai
6. See the master list on page 282.

THE WILDERNESS WANDERINGS
Worksheet
1. c. 1446–1406 B.C.
2. Numbers 9–20
3. They did not trust the Lord to take care of them.
4. Water—water from a rock; food—manna; meat—birds
5. twelve
6. two
7. They had to wander in the wilderness for 40 years.
8. A cloud by day and a fiery pillar by night
9. They died.

Project 1
The spies brought back a branch of grapes, pomegranates, and figs.
The spies scouted for forty days.
Some scouts said the Canaanites were giants.
The Israelites wished they had died in Egypt and some considered going back.
The people sought to stone Joshua and Caleb.
The Glory of the Lord appeared and wanted to kill all the people, but Moses interceded for them.
Everyone 20 years and older would die in the wilderness.
The spies who brought back the report died by a plague before the Lord.
Some Israelites attempted to take the land but were defeated.

Test
1. c. 1446–1406 B.C.
2. Numbers 9–20
3. Water, food, meat
4. See what the land was like
5. Joshua and Caleb
6. They had to wander in the wilderness for 40 years.
7. A cloud by day and a fiery pillar by night
8. They died.

ANSWERS

Review
1. God would make him a great nation.
2. Abraham, Isaac, Jacob, Judah
3. He parted the Red Sea so that the Israelites could cross on dry ground. Then he let the waters fall back on the Egyptian army.
4. The "finger" of God
5. He threw down the stone tablets and they broke.
6. See the master list on page 282.

BALAAM AND HIS DONKEY
Worksheet
1. c. 1406 B.C.
2. Numbers 22–24
3. The Israelites were numerous.
4. Balaam
5. He was a prophet who was evil and sold his services to the highest bidder.
6. An angel
7. It could see the angel.
8. The ability to talk
9. He could only bless them.

Project 1
1. Balak
2. The LORD
3. Donkey
4. Balaam
5. Balak
6. Balaam

Test
1. c. 1406 B.C.
2. Numbers 22–24
3. The Israelites were numerous.
4. Balaam was to curse Israel.
5. He was a prophet who was evil and sold his services to the highest bidder.
6. To stop Balaam from cursing Israel
7. It sat down.
8. The ability to talk
9. He could only bless them

Review
1. 1. You shall have no other gods before me. 2. You shall not make for yourself a carved image. 3. You shall not take the name of the Lord your God in vain. 4. Remember the Sabbath day to keep it holy. 5. Honor your father and mother. 6. You shall not murder. 7. You shall not commit adultery. 8. You shall not steal. 9. You shall not bear false witness against your neighbor. 10. You shall not covet.
2. See the master list on page 282.

MOSES DIES;
JOSHUA ASSUMES COMMAND
Worksheet
1. c. 1406 B.C.
2. Deuteronomy 34
3. He had disobeyed God by not believing his word.
4. Mt. Nebo
5. God took it and buried it.
6. Joshua
7. Salvation
8. To show them that God had chosen Joshua to be their leader

Project 1
Moses saw the promised land from Mt. Nebo.
Moses was not allowed to cross over to the promised land.
God buried Moses.
The Israelites mourned for Moses for thirty days.
Moses had lain hands on Joshua so he took command.
No prophet knew the Lord face to face like Moses did.

Test
1. c. 1406 B.C.
2. Deuteronomy 34
3. He was not allowed to enter the Promised Land.
4. He looked over into the Promised Land.
5. God
6. Be the new leader of the Israelites
7. Salvation
8. Moses told them Joshua was God's choice.

ANSWERS

Review
1. Arabs
2. They were to be sacrificed to God.
3. 40 days
4. The Most Holy Place
5. The Levites
6. See the master list on page 282.

SPIES TO CANAAN
Worksheet
1. c. 1406 B.C.
2. Joshua 2
3. Jericho
4. Rahab's house
5. They had heard how God plagued Egypt in order to free them.
6. Rahab hid them.
7. She and her family were spared.
8. Boaz

Project
1. On the roof with stalks of flax.
2. God's parting of the Red Sea.
3. Tie a scarlet cord in her window.

Test
1. c. 1406 B.C.
2. Joshua 2
3. To gather information about the city
4. The people of Jericho were afraid of the Israelites.
5. She hid them.
6. She was a prostitute.
7. She and her family were spared.
8. Boaz is Rahab's son.

Review
1. A golden calf
2. The Ten Commandments, Aaron's staff, and a jar of manna
3. Jesus
4. Two
5. 40
6. See the master list on page 282.

THE BATTLE OF JERICHO
Worksheet
1. c. 1406 B.C.
2. Joshua 5:13–6:27
3. That the battle for the Promised Land belonged to the Lord and not Joshua's army
4. March around the city
5. They marched around the city seven times. Then the priests blew their trumpets and the men gave out a cry.
6. God knocked down the walls.
7. Rahab
8. Rahab had tied a red ribbon in her window.

Project 1
4/6/2/8/3/5/1/9/7

Test
1. c. 1406 B.C.
2. Joshua 5:13–6:27
3. The commander of the army of heaven
4. Seven
5. The ark of the covenant
6. The priests blew their trumpets, and the men gave a shout.
7. God knocked down the walls.
8. Their lives were spared.

Review
1. Live in the land of Goshen
2. They were numerous, and he was afraid of their numbers.
3. Answers will vary.
4. A priest is one who stands between God and man.
5. Curse the Israelites
6. See the master list on page 282.

ISRAEL GIVEN THE PROMISED LAND
Worksheet
1. c. 1400–1350 B.C.
2. Joshua 21:43–45; Judges 1:8–36
3. God enabled them.
4. They did not drive out or destroy the Canaanites as they were commanded.
5. Live among them or pay tribute to them
6. They tempted Israel to follow after their false gods.
7. Judah

Answers

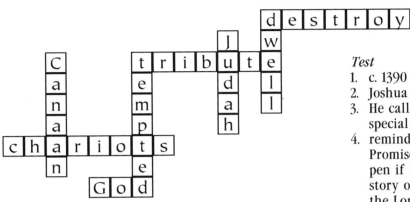

Test
1. c. 1400–1350 B.C.
2. Joshua 21:43–45; Judges 1:8–36
3. God
4. drive out or destroy the Canaanites
5. They allowed them to live among them or pay tribute.
6. Follow after false gods
7. Judah

Review
1. Rainbow
2. She was turned into a pillar of salt.
3. Joshua
4. Answers will vary.
5. Rahab
6. See the master list on page 282.

Joshua's Last Words

Worksheet
1. c. 1390 B.C.
2. Joshua 23, 24
3. To give them a special message
4. reminded them of God's blessing them with the Promised Land, warned them of what would happen if they broke the covenant, recounted the story of Israel, pleaded with them to not forsake the Lord.
5. God would curse and destroy them.
6. They became witnesses that they would follow after the Lord.

Project 1
fought land LORD marriages hearts promised covenant anger tribes Canaan Jacob Esau Moses chariots Red bless plant gods Egypt gods covenant Joshua Joseph

Test
1. c. 1390 B.C.
2. Joshua 23, 24
3. He called all of the tribes to him to give them a special message.
4. reminded them of God's blessing them with the Promised Land, warned them of what would happen if they broke the covenant, recounted the story of Israel, pleaded with them to not forsake the Lord.
5. God would curse and destroy them.
6. They became witnesses that they would follow after the Lord.

Review
1. Water, food, meat
2. His donkey spoke.
3. March around the city
4. A red ribbon
5. Judah
6. See the master list on page 282.

ANSWERS

GENESIS-JOSHUA BIBLE CARDS *Master List*

Creation | *Genesis 1-2*
The Fall in the Garden | *Genesis 3*
Cain and Abel | *Genesis 4*
Enoch and Methuselah | *Genesis 5:21-32*
The Flood | *Genesis 6-9*
God's Covenant with Noah | *Genesis 9:1-17*
Tower of Babel | *Genesis 11*
Call of Abram | *Genesis 12, 13* | c. 2091 B.C.
God's Covenant with Abraham |
    Genesis 15-17 | c. 2082 B.C.
Hagar and Ishmael | *Genesis 16, 21* | c. 2080 B.C.
Sodom and Gomorrah | *Genesis 18-19* | c. 2080 B.C.
Birth and Sacrifice of Isaac | *Genesis 21-22* | 2066 B.C.
Isaac and Rebekah | *Genesis 24* | c. 2026 B.C.
Jacob and Esau | *Genesis 25:19-34; 27:1-46* | c. 2000 B.C.
Joseph as a Slave | *Genesis 37-40* | c. 1898 B.C.
Famine in Egypt | *Genesis 41-47* | c. 1878-1871 B.C.
The Twelve Tribes of Israel |
    Genesis 29-36, 46-50 | c. 1860 B.C.
Moses' Birth | *Exodus 1-2* | c. 1525 B.C.
Plagues in Egypt | *Exodus 3-12* | c. 1446 B.C.
The Exodus | *Exodus 13-15* | c. 1446 B.C.
Ten Commandments | *Exodus 19-20* | c. 1445 B.C.
Aaron and the Golden Calf | *Exodus 32* | c. 1444 B.C.
Moses Gets New Tablets | *Exodus 34* | 1444 B.C.
The Tabernacle and the Ark of the Covenant |
    Exodus 36-37 | c. 1444-1435 B.C.
The Levitical Priesthood Begins |
    Numbers 3 | c. 1440 B.C.
The Wilderness Wanderings |
    Numbers 9-20 | c. 1446-1406 B.C.
Balaam and His Donkey |
    Numbers 22-24 | c. 1406 B.C.
Moses Dies; Joshua Assumes Command |
    Deuteronomy 34 | c. 1406 B.C.
Spies to Canaan | *Joshua 2* | c. 1406 B.C.
The Battle of Jericho | *Joshua 5:13-6:27* | c. 1406 B.C.
Israel Given the Promised Land |
    Joshua 21:43-45; Judges 1:8-36 | c. 1400-1350 B.C.
Joshua's Last Words | *Joshua 23, 24* | c. 1390 B.C.

Creation

Project 2—Mural

Make a mural depicting what was created on each day. Divide a large sheet of paper into six sections. Label each section Day 1, Day 2, Day 3, etc. Have students search magazines for pictures or cut out parts of pictures of things that God created. Glue the pictures in the appropriate section of the mural. Students may make individual murals or work together to make a giant class mural.

 © Copyright 2001, Veritas Press | 800-922-5082

Worksheet

1. What is the Scripture reference for this card?
2. Was there ever a time when God did not exist?
3. Who created the world and all that is in it?
4. In how many days was the world created?
5. List what was created or done on each day.

Project 1—Bible Reading

Read this story in Genesis 1. Unscramble the words below on the left and then draw a line to connect the words with the phrases on the right that go with them.

Kandesrs   God told the creatures to _____ and fill the earth.

HIgit   God saw that everything was _____.

Ultylimp   _____ face of the deep. _____ was on the

Gamei   God made man in his own _____.

Oniondim   God said, "Let there be _____."

Mimatrenf   God told man to have _____ over the earth.

Odog   The _____ divided the waters above from the waters below.

Project 2—Cherubim

Ezekiel describes cherubim as having four faces, four wings and cloven feet. In Revelation they are covered with eyes and have six wings and combined the likeness of a lion, ox, eagle and a man. Monstrous scultures of this sort were fashioned in Egypt and Asyria (the example of cherubim above was found at the Palace of Konyunjik). In the New Testament, the messengers of God appear as young men, bright as lightning.

Make a clay model of a cherubim like the ones God put in the Garden of Eden to guard the Tree of Life. Refer to Genesis 3:24 to find what weapon the cherubim had for this job.

The Fall

© Copyright 2001, Veritas Press | 800-922-5082

Worksheet

1. What is the Scripture reference for this card?

2. How did the devil disguise himself when he came to Eve?

3. What did the devil tempt Eve to do?

4. What did Adam do when Eve gave the fruit to him?

5. What had God told Adam about the fruit of the Tree of Knowledge?

6. What did God curse because of Adam and Eve's sin?

7. How had man's relationship with God changed?

Project 1—Bible Reading

Read Genesis 3 to find the answers to the following:

1. The deceiver was the _____.

2. Eve and Adam ate _____.

3. They sewed _____ into coverings.

4. After Adam and Eve sinned they _____ from God.

5. The serpent was cursed to crawl on his _____.

6. Eve would have great _____ in bearing children.

7. Adam would have to _____ for food and the ground would bring forth _____ and _____.

8. God made Adam and Eve _____ to wear.

9. God drove them out of the Garden and placed _____ to guard it.

Project 2

Make fancy letters to spell out the names of Cain and/or Abel. Each letter should include something that has to do with the person. The name should be written vertically, and next to each letter write a sentence explaining how its design relates to the person. Below is an example of how you might write Eve's name.

Eve lived with Adam in the Garden of Eden.

The serpent tempted Eve.

Eve ate the fruit of the Tree of Knowledge.

Cain and Abel

© Copyright 2001, Veritas Press | 800-922-5082

Worksheet

1. What is the Scripture reference for this card?

2. Who was the first child of Adam and Eve?

3. What job did Cain do?

4. What job did Abel do?

5. What offering did Cain bring to God?

6. What offering did Abel bring to God?

7. With whose offering was God pleased?

8. Which son murdered his brother?

Project 1—Bible Reading

Read Genesis 4. Using your Bible find who said each quote below. Write their names in the blanks. The quotes are listed in the order in which they occurred in the story.

1. "I have acquired a man from the Lord." _____

2. "Why are you angry, and why has your countenance fallen?" _____

3. "Where is Abel your brother?" _____

4. "Am I my brother's keeper?" _____

5. "I shall be a fugitive and a vagabond on the earth, and it will happen that anyone who finds me will kill me." _____

6. "Therefore, whoever kills Cain, vengeance shall be taken on him sevenfold." _____

Project 2—Graphing

People lived a lot longer in the days before Noah. Methuselah lived the longest of all people that the Bible records. Fill in the chart with the ages of Adam and his godly line. Use the Bible references to look up each man's age. Each verse is located in Genesis 5.

Ages of Adam's Godly Line to Methuselah

NAME	AGE
Adam (v5)	
Seth (v8)	
Enosh (v11)	
Kenan (v14)	
Mahalel (v17)	
Jared (v20)	
Enoch (v23)	
Methuselah (v27)	

Enoch and
Methuselah

 © Copyright 2001, Veritas Press | 800-922-5082

Worksheet

1. What is the Scripture reference for this card?

2. Who was the godly child that Adam and Eve had after Cain murdered Abel?

3. Enoch's life was characterized by consistent

   _____ and _____.

4. What did the Lord do for Enoch since he was so pleased with Enoch?

5. Enoch is the _____ generation after Adam in _____ godly line.

6. What does the number seven represent in the Scriptures?

7. How is Methuselah related to Enoch?

8. What was special about Methuselah?

9. How is Methuselah related to Noah?

Project 1—Bible Reading

Read Genesis 5:21–32 and fill in the timeline. Can you calculate how many years are between Enoch and Methuselah's deaths?

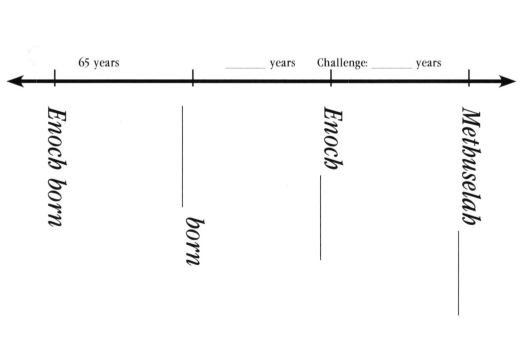

Methuselah _____

Enoch _____

Challenge: _____ years   _____ years

_____ born

65 years

Enoch born

The Flood

Project 2—Talk to the Animals

Pretend you are interviewing animals that came off the ark. Write the animal's answers on the lines provided.

Reporter: Mr. Monkey, how did you get inside that big boat?
MONKEY: _____
_____

Reporter: Mr. Skunk, some animals don't like your smell.
Why weren't you lonely on the ark?
SKUNK: _____
_____

Reporter: Mr. Raven, you had a pretty important job.
What did you do?
RAVEN: _____
_____

Reporter: Mr. Pig you were quite fortunate to not be
sacrificed like each of the clean animals when Noah got
off the ark. What did you see in the sky to promise that the
earth would never be flooded again?
PIG: _____
_____

© Copyright 2001, Veritas Press | 800-922-5082

Worksheet

1. What is the Scripture reference for this card?

2. What did God observe about man?

3. Who found grace in the eyes of the Lord?

4. What was to be put in the ark?

5. How long did it rain?

6. What happened to all of the people except Noah and his family?

7. What did God promise Noah after the flood?

8. What sign of the covenant did God give?

Project 1—Bible Reading

Read the account of the Flood in Genesis. Then fill in the text and crossword puzzle on the next page.

Across

1. God told Noah to build an ark out of _____.

5. The ark settled after the flood on the mountains of _____.

6. Noah first sent a _____ out of the ark.

7. The second dove came back with an olive _____ in her mouth.

Down

2. Noah covered the ark with _____.

3. The ark had _____ decks.

4. Noah took _____ of each of the clean animals.

6. God made the _____ a sign that he wouldn't flood the earth again.

8. The first thing Noah built when he left the ark was an _____.

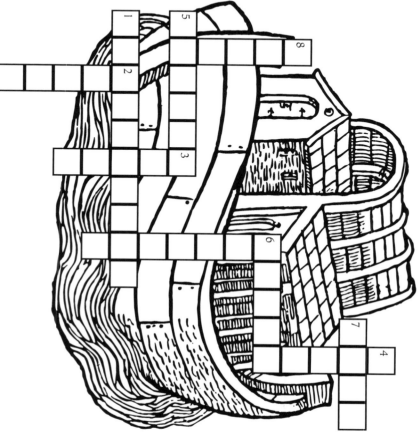

Project 2

The colors of the rainbow are red, orange, yellow, green, blue, indigo, and violet. Use the letters ROYGBIV to write words or phrases that have to do with Noah's Ark and God's Covenant with Noah. Begin each word or phrase with a letter for the colors of the rainbow.

R	
O	
Y	
G	
B	
I	
V	

God's Covenant with Noah

© Copyright 2001, Veritas Press | 800-922-5082

Worksheet

1. What is the Scripture reference for this card?

2. A _____ is like a promise.

3. Who participated in the first covenant that is described in the Bible?

4. What did God promise to Noah and his descendants?

5. What was the sign that God gave Noah to confirm his covenant?

6. What did Noah remember every time he saw the sign of the covenant?

Project 1—Bible Reading

Read Genesis 9:1-17. In the basket on the left draw examples of what Noah was allowed to eat before the Flood and on the right draw examples of what we are allowed to eat now. Then color the picture, adding the missing sign of God's covenant.

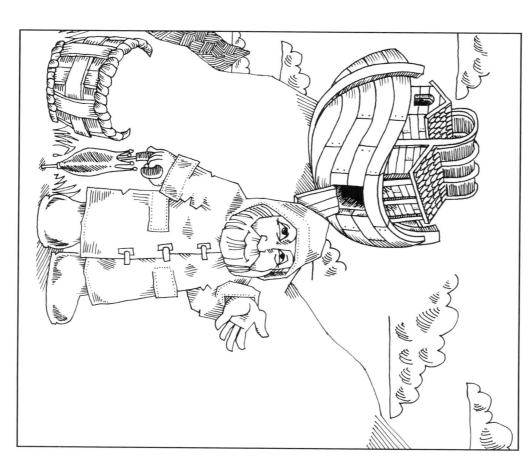

The Tower of Babel

Project 2–Biblical art study

Pieter Bruegel (about 1525-69), usually known as Pieter Bruegel the Elder or "Peasant Bruegel" due to his subjects: peasant life, proverbs and New Testament topics set among common folks of contemporary Flanders.

Bruegel the Elder's paintings are full of zest and fine detail while they expose human weaknesses and follies. Bruegel's art is often seen as the last phase in the development of a long tradition of Netherlandish painting beginning with Jan van Eyck in the 15th century.

Discuss Bruegel's painting *The Tower of Babel.*

1. How is the confusion of Babel shown in the construction of the building?

2. What is Nimrod doing in the painting (lower left)?

3. What classic Roman building seems to be the inspiration for Bruegel's nonsensical tower?

 © Copyright 2001, Veritas Press | 800-922-5082

Worksheet

1. What is the Scripture reference for this card?

2. How many languages were spoken on earth before the Tower of Babel was built?

3. Of what did the people become proud?

4. How did God curse the people because of their pride?

5. What is the tower that some people believe may be the Tower of Babel?

Project 1—Bible Reading

Read Genesis 11 and complete these statements.

1. The whole earth spoke one _____ .

2. They made _____ of stone and _____ for mortar.

3. They set out to build a _____ and a _____ whose top was in the _____ .

4. The Lord came down and _____ their language and _____ them all over the face of the earth.

5. This place is called _____ .

Project

To the right of each arrow write a description or draw a picture of Abram's life after he followed God's call.

ABRAM'S LIFE IN UR: *AFTER GOD CALLED ABRAM:*

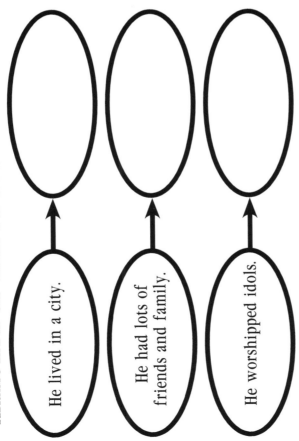

He lived in a city. →

He had lots of friends and family. →

He worshipped idols. →

Call of Abram

 © Copyright 2001, Veritas Press | 800-922-5082

Worksheet

1. What is the date for the call of Abram?

2. What is the Scripture reference for the call of Abram?

3. Where was Abram's home?

4. Who was Abram's wife?

5. Who went with Abram?

6. Where did Abram settle?

7. What did God tell Abram about the land in which he had settled?

Project 1—Bible Reading

After reading Genesis 12, 13 you will learn two stories that occurred during Abram's journey. Complete the word find on the next page, but be sure to know what each word has to do with the two events during Abram's journey.

```
C A N N A A N I T E S A D D L D
S E P A R A T E N E D C I V A E
P H A R O A C A N A A N I T E S
A N T S A R A I Q W E L R T Y C
B U L I V E S T O C K S T A R E
D B R S E N D A E N M B V A C N
S L U T E G Y P T N S I S T R D
T E R E B I N T H X T R E E S A
P A B R S E L K J H G S F D T N
H L O T J S A S S F L O C K S T
A Z A S X O S U C U A M N B V S
R S L G J S R S T H N M S S S F
A A E A U T R D S I O D I S S L
O R S L O E E W A S F O A N S U
H A T T C S S L A N D U L Y E K
V H W A K P H A R O A H L I N E
```

Egypt	Sarai	Descendants
Famine	Livestock	Terebinth trees
Pharaoh	Lot	Altar
Sister	Tents	Land
Beautiful	Flocks	Canaanites
Plagues	Separate	
Abram	Jordan	

God's Covenant
with Abraham

Project

*Explain what each picture
has to do with God's covenant ,
then color the pictures.*

© Copyright 2001, Veritas Press | 800-922-5082

Worksheet

1. What is the date for God's covenant with Abraham?

2. What is the Scripture reference for God's covenant with Abraham?

3. What did God promise Abraham?

4. When God made his covenant with Abraham, Sarah and Abraham were too old to have what?

5. What animals did Abraham cut in two pieces?

6. In what form did the Lord move between the pieces of the dead animals?

7. What sign did God later give to Abraham?

Project 1—Bible Reading

Read Genesis 15 and use your Bible to fill in the blanks.

THE PROMISE:

1. God promised Abram many _____ that would outnumber the _____.

2. God also promised to give Abram _____.

CONFIRMATION OF THE PROMISE:

1. Abram cut _____ and _____, along with a pigeon and turtledove opposite each other.

2. Abram had to chase away _____.

3. God told Abram that his descendants would serve another nation for _____ years. Then they would leave that land with great _____ and return to this _____ which God was promising Abram.

4. A _____ and a _____ passed between the pieces.

THE SIGN OF THE COVENANT:

1. Genesis 17:10 Every male child was to be _____.

THE NAME CHANGES:

1. Genesis 17:5 Abram's name changed to _____.

2. Genesis 17:15 Sarai's name changed to _____.

Hagar and Ishmael

Project 2

Put the words at the bottom of the page under the woman to which they go in the story.

SARAH   HAGAR

_____   _____

_____   _____

_____   _____

_____   _____

_____   _____

maidservant | Isaac | Ishmael | Arabs | ran away
treated the other harshly | Sarai | 90
scoffed at a feast of weaning | visited by an angel

© Copyright 2001, Veritas Press | 800-922-5082

Worksheet

1. What is the date for Hagar and Ishmael?

2. What is the Scripture reference for Hagar and Ishmael?

3. What had Sarah not been able to give to Abraham?

4. Why did Abraham marry Hagar?

5. How did Sarah treat Hagar when she found out Hagar was going to have a baby?

6. What did the Angel tell Hagar about her descendants?

7. What did Abraham do to Hagar when she scoffed at Isaac's feast?

8. What modern day people are believed to be the descendants of Ishmael?

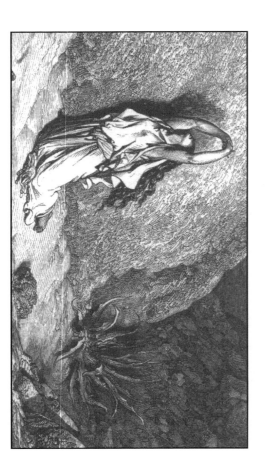

Project 1—Bible Reading

Read Genesis 16, 21 and then complete the word find below.
Be sure to know what each word has to do with they story.

```
W I A S W W S S H A G A R N M M
I S E A I S H M A E L F H O L A
L H L S L T S S R S S S L A P K I
D F L E D R D E S P I S E D J D
E M D S E S S S H H S A G W I S
R C C B R K Q R T A S R A A H E
N H E I N I F U X R S A S T G R
S I G F E N S V B S B I R E F V
A L J H S S U O O H O R S R E A
R D K I S P S A E I W A A S D N
A L R N S S R B A C S E S K S T
H E S S L M S I S S H S A I C B
Q S D T A U V W N S O X Y N Z A
P S N M R L K J I G T H G F E E
O P Q R A R C H E R S T U V W D
S N M L I K J I H G F E D C B A
```

childless	fled	weaned
maidservant	spring	waterskin
Hagar	wilderness	bowshot
despised	Ishmael	archer
harsh	Sarai	

Project 2

Diorama Supplies

1' SQUARE PIECE OF
CARDBOARD (you can also
put diorama inside a
shoebox)

SMALL BOXES (jello, film,
medicine size),

CARDBOARD TUBES

TISSUE PAPER: red, orange,
and yellow

GLUE

PIPE CLEANERS

SALT

CLAY

CONSTRUCTION PAPER

SCISSORS

BLACK MARKER

YARN

FELT, FABRIC

Directions

Paint the small boxes and tubes a sand color. These will be arranged to be buildings of the cities. When the paint is dry use black marker to draw on windows, doors, and other details. Use construction paper to add more details to the cities. Glue the two cities to the cardboard square. Make people by folding 4" pieces of pipe cleaners in half. The crease of the fold is the head. Separate the bottom ends to make legs. Attach another 1" pipe cleaner to make arms. Using paper, fabric and/or felt glue clothes to the pipe cleaner bodies. Use clay and other supplies to make parcels. Yarn can be glued on as hair. Use glue or clay to attach people to the cardboard base. Make a thin pillar out of clay, cover it with glue, and pour salt on it to make Lot's wife.

Sodom and Gomorrah

© Copyright 2001, Veritas Press | 800-922-5082

Worksheet

1. What is the date for Sodom and Gomorrah?

2. What is the Scripture reference for Sodom and Gomorrah?

3. What did God plan to do to Sodom and Gomorrah?

4. What would God have done if there were ten righteous men living in Sodom and Gomorrah?

5. Who was the only righteous man in those cities?

6. What foolish thing did the wife of the righteous man do?

7. What happened to the wife of the righteous man?

8. What did this event teach Abraham and his descendants?

Project 1—Bible Reading

Read about this story in The Child's Story Bible pages 23, 24. Then answer the following questions:

1. Explain how the two angels saved Lot when the wicked people came to his house.

   _____

2. Where did Lot go after he fled from Sodom and Gomorrah?

   _____

   _____

3. Who was with Lot after he left the cities?

   _____

   _____

   _____

The Birth and Sacrifice of Isaac

Project 2—Bible Reading

Read Genesis 22 and put these events in order from 1-11.

___ Abraham, Isaac, & some men went to the mountains at Moriah.

___ The Angel of the Lord stopped Abraham.

___ Abraham sacrificed the ram.

___ God told Abraham to sacrifice Isaac.

___ Abraham said that God would provide the offering.

___ Abraham named the place The-Lord-Will-Provide.

___ Abraham built an altar and put wood on it.

___ Abraham told his men that they were going away to worship and would return soon.

___ Isaac was bound to the altar.

___ God promised Abraham again to make his descendants numerous.

___ Abraham took his knife to slay Isaac.

 © Copyright 2001, Veritas Press | 800-922-5082

Worksheet

Down

1. What is the date for the birth and sacrifice of Isaac?
2. What is the Scripture reference for the birth and sacrifice of Isaac?
3. How old were Abraham and Sarah when they had Isaac?
4. What did God command Abraham to do to Isaac?
5. On what mountain did Abraham build the altar?
6. Who stopped Abraham from sacrificing Isaac?
7. What did Abraham really sacrifice on the altar?
8. What about Abraham pleased God?

Down

4. God provided a _____ to be sacrificed instead of Abraham's son.
5. Where did Abraham find what he actually sacrificed?
6. A sacrifice was placed on an _____ of Abraham.
7. God was pleased with the _____.
8. What did God tell Abraham to do to his son?
9. What about Abraham and Sarah made Isaac's birth mircaulous?

Project 1—Crossword Puzzle

Across

1. On what mountain did Abraham take his son?
2. What stopped Abraham from sacrificing his son?
3. Whom did God tell Abraham to sacrifice?

Review

1. List what was created or done on each day.
   Day 1 _____
   Day 2 _____
   Day 3 _____
   Day 4 _____
   Day 5 _____
   Day 6 _____
   Day 7 _____
2. Who was the first child of Adam and Eve?
3. What is a covenant?
4. What were the people of the earth trying to build that would reach the heavens?
5. Who was Abraham's wife?
6. What would God have done if there had been ten righteous men living in Sodom and Gomorrah?

Isaac and Rebekah

© Copyright 2001, Veritas Press | 800-922-5082

Worksheet

1. What is the date for this card?

2. What is the Scripture reference for this card?

3. Whom did Abraham send to find a bride for his son?

4. By what sign would the servant know that this was the right girl?

5. Who was the girl that the servant found?

6. The girl was Isaac's _____ .

7. When did the girl leave with Abraham's?

Project 1—Bible Reading

After reading Genesis 24, complete the following questions.

1. In those days you did not put your hand on the Bible to swear an oath. Where did Abraham's servant put his hand to swear the oath? (Genesis 24:9)

2. What did the servant give to Rebekah after she watered his camels? (Gen 24:22)

   _____

3. Until when wouldn't the servant eat? (Gen 24:33)

   _____

4. For how many days did Rebekah's brother and mother ask the servant to stay before going back with her? (Genesis 24:55)

   _____

5. Who decided that Rebekah would go back with the servant immediately? (Genesis 24:58)

   _____

Project 2–Middle Eastern Lentil Soup

Esau sold his birthright for a bowl of soup. Here is a soup recipe that, though good, probably won't make anyone want to give up his birthright. Makes 4 servings.

1 cup dried lentils	2 tbls olive oil
1 onion, chopped	1 red bell pepper, chopped
1 tsp fennel seed	1/4 tsp ground red pepper
1/2 tsp ground cumin	1 tbl lemon juice
1/2 tsp salt	

1. Rinse lentils, discarding any blemished lentils; drain.
2. Heat oil in large saucepan over medium-high heat until hot. Add onion and bell pepper; cook and stir 5 minutes or until tender. Add cumin, fennel seed and ground red pepper; cook and stir 1 minute.
3. Add 4 cups water and lentils. Bring to a boil. Reduce heat to low. Cover and simmer 20 minutes. Stir in salt. Simmer 5 to 10 minutes more or until lentils are tender. Stir in lemon juice. For a special touch, top each serving with yellow bell pepper strips.

Jacob and Esau

© Copyright 2001, Veritas Press | 800-922-5082

Worksheet

1. What is the date for this card?

2. What is the Scripture reference for this card?

3. What did God tell Rebekah about the twins she would have?

4. The firstborn son was named _____.

5. The name "Jacob" means _____.

6. What is a birthright?

7. For what did Esau sell his birthright?

8. Isaac was old and _____.

9. Even though Esau had foolishly sold his birthright, what did Isaac still determine to do?

10. How did Isaac try to be sure that the son he was blessing was Esau?

11. How did Jacob trick his father?

Project 1—Bible Reading

1. Read Genesis 25:19-34, 27:1-46. Write a sentence using each of the words below, explaining its use in the story.

heel
_____

lentils
_____

smooth-skinned
_____

blind
_____

2. What did Esau plan to do after his father died?
_____
_____

3. Who overheard Esau's plan?
_____
_____
_____

Joseph as a Slave

Project 2

Draw a picture of one time in which Joseph was in bondage.

© Copyright 2001, Veritas Press | 800-922-5082

Worksheet

1. What is the date for Joseph as a Slave?

2. What is the Scripture reference for Joseph as a Slave?

3. What did Joseph dream when he was seventeen?

4. Why did Joseph's brothers envy him?

5. What did Joseph's brothers conspire to do?

6. Who convinced his brothers to put Joseph into a pit?

7. To whom was Joseph sold?

8. What was done to Joseph's coat so his father would think he was dead?

9. How did Joseph end up in prison?

Project 1—Bible Reading

In Genesis 40 we read of Joseph's days in prison. How did Joseph first become a slave? How did Joseph then become imprisoned? In prison he interpreted the dreams of Pharaoh's chief butler and chief baker. *Draw pictures illustrating what each man saw in his dream. In the space below, write Joseph's interpretation of each dream. Were Joseph's interpretations correct?*

Butler

Baker

Project 2—Family Tree

Pharaoh invited Joseph's family to come and live in Egypt.
Using your knowledge of the patriarchs, complete the
following family tree on another piece of paper.

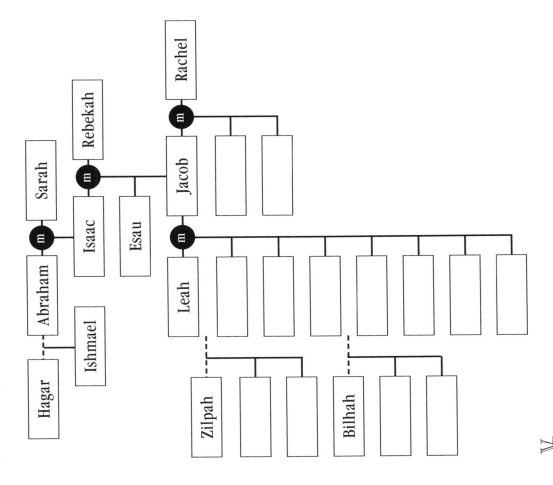

Famine in Egypt

© Copyright 2001, Veritas Press | 800-922-5082

Worksheet

1. What is the date for the famine in Egypt?

2. What is the Scripture reference for the famine in Egypt?

3. Who told Pharaoh of Joseph's ability to interpret dreams?

4. Whom did Joseph say gave him the ability to interpret Pharaoh's dreams?

5. What did Pharaoh's dream indicate would happen in the future?

6. What high position did Pharaoh give Joseph for interpreting his dream?

7. Who came to Egypt to buy grain?

8. What did Pharaoh invite Jacob and his family to do?

Project 1—Bible Reading

Read Genesis 37 and answer the following questions:

1. In Pharaoh's dream, what did the seven gaunt cows represent?

   _____

   _____

2. Name the gifts that Pharaoh gave Joseph when he made him second-in-command.

   _____

   _____

3. What did Joseph at first accuse his brothers of being when they first came to Egypt for his help?

   _____

   _____

   _____

Twelve Tribes of Israel

Project 2—Twelve Tribes Mobile

Color the pictures of each of the 12 sons of Jacob. Cut them out and glue the backs of the sons of Leah to one color of construction paper. Glue the backs of the sons of Rachel, Zilpah, & Bilhah to different colors of construction paper. Trim the construction paper along the edges of the pictures. With a hole punch put a hole in the top of each picture. Cut 12 foot-long lengths of string. Tie one end of each string to the hole of a picture and the other end to a clothes hanger. Make two paper namecards, one reading Jacob and the other reading Israel. Tape one just under the hook of the hanger. Glue the second namecard to the back of the first.

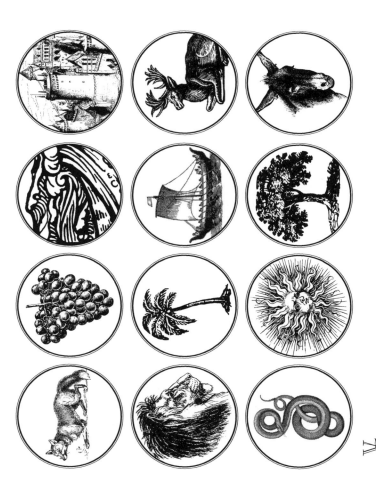

© Copyright 2001, Veritas Press | 800-922-5082

Worksheet

1. What is the date for the twelve tribes of Israel?

2. What is the Scripture reference for the twelve tribes of Israel?

3. What had God promised to Abraham?

4. Name the three Patriarchs.

5. To what did God change Jacob's name?

6. How many sons did Jacob have?

7. What are the descendents of Jacob's sons known as?

Project 1—Bible Reading

In Genesis 49 Jacob gives his final words to his sons. He tells about his sons' past and prophesies about their futures. He also identifies many of them with a symbol or animal. Each tribe has a symbol to represent it. (For a complete illustration of the tribal symbols see the *Children's Illustrated Bible*, p. 89.) Draw one of the tribal symbols below and label it with the name of the tribe.

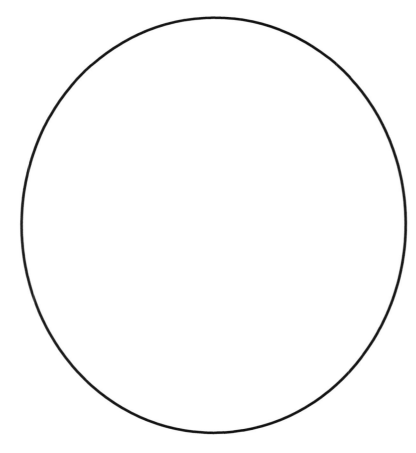

Moses' Birth

Review

1. What was Noah to take into the ark with him?
2. What did God promise to Abraham?
3. Why did Abraham marry Hagar?
4. How was Rebekah related to Isaac? (other than being his wife)
5. What did Jacob do so that Isaac would think he was giving the blessing to Esau?
6. What did Joseph's brothers do so that their father would think Joseph was dead?

 © Copyright 2001, Veritas Press | 800-922-5082

Worksheet

1. What is the date for the birth of Moses?

2. What is the Scripture reference for the birth of Moses?

3. What did the new Pharaoh fear about the Israelites?

4. What did Pharaoh do to the Israelites?

5. What did Pharaoh order the midwives to do?

6. What did the Levite couple do to save their son?

7. Who found the Levite baby?

8. What does the name Moses mean?

Project 1—Bible Reading

Read the acount of Moses' birth in Genesis, then fill in the crossword puzzle below.

Down

1. Pharaoh feared the numerous Israelites so he made them _____.

2. The name _____ means "to draw out".

3. Moses' parents were from the tribe of _____.

6. Egyptian women were _____ in the river near the basket.

Across

2. Pharaoh ordered them to kill Israelite boys when they were born.

4. Moses was put in a basket in the _____ River.

5. Moses' _____ hid along the river to watch the baby.

7. The _____ of Pharaoh found the baby in the river.

8. Moses' own mother was paid to _____ him for the princess.

It took Pharaoh quite a bit of convincing to let the Israelites go. But when God was through with him he had good reason—ten of them! Make a poster illustrating the top ten reasons the Israelites should be freed. On another sheet of paper illustrate and label each reason why the Israelites should go. Each plague would have been another reason to get rid of the Israelites. You may number the plagues in the order in which they occurred. Or you may number the first plague as number ten and count down to the number one reason—the killing of the firstborn.

Plagues in Egypt

 © Copyright 2001, Veritas Press | 800-922-5082

Worksheet

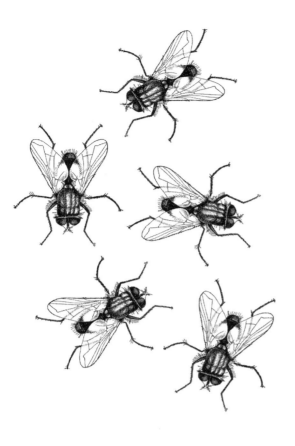

1. What is the date for the Plagues in Egypt?

2. What is the Scripture reference for the Plagues in Egypt?

3. Through what did God speak to Moses?

4. What did God tell Moses to do for the Israelites?

5. Who went with Moses to Pharaoh?

6. What did Moses request from Pharaoh?

7. What did God send each time Pharaoh refused Moses' request?

8. Each plague was an attack on what?

Project 1—Bible Reading

Read Exodus 3 and write a paragraph explaining Moses' experience with the burning bush.

_____

_____

_____

_____

_____

_____

_____

_____

_____

_____

_____

_____

_____

_____

_____

_____

_____

_____

The Exodus

Project 2–Diorama

Supplies

Clay or play dough: blue, brown, and green
Sand
1' square piece of cardboard
paper people and chariot cutouts

Directions

Make a diorama depicting the parting of the Red Sea. Choose any part of the crossing to depict. Form clay into the parted waters on top of the cardboard square. You may want to make ground from clay and/or sand on either side of their Red Sea. Color and cut out paper figures representing the Pillar of Fire, Moses, the Israelites and the Egyptians. Place them on the diorama.

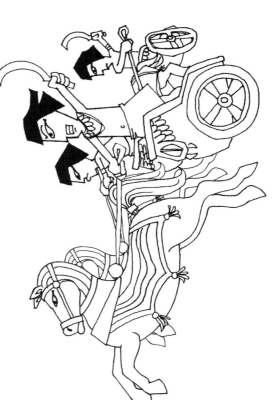

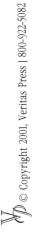 © Copyright 2001, Veritas Press | 800-922-5082

Worksheet

1. What is the date for the Exodus?

2. What is the Scripture reference for the Exodus?

3. What was the tenth plague on Egypt?

4. How were the Israelites spared from the tenth plague?

5. What special day of the Israelites remembers God's sparing them from the tenth plague?

6. Where did the Israelites camp after leaving Egypt?

7. What did Pharaoh do when he changed his mind?

8. How did God save the Israelites from the Egyptians?

Project 1—Bible Reading

Read the account of the Red Sea crossing in Exodus 14. Use each phrase below in a sentence that relates to this story. For example: . . . silver, gold, and clothing . . . The Israelites left Egypt taking along Egyptian silver, gold, and clothing.

. . . PURSUED THE ISRAELITES . . .

_____

_____

. . . CAMPING BY THE SEA . . . .

_____

_____

. . . STRETCHED OUT HIS HANDS . . . .

_____

_____

. . . PILLAR OF CLOUD . . .

_____

_____

. . . CHARIOTS AND HORSEMEN . . .

_____

_____

Ten Commandments

Project 2

The Ten Commandments are known for being negative "Thou Shalt Nots." Read the Westminster Shorter Catechism questions 42, 46, 50, 54, 58, 60, 64, 68, 71, 74, 77, and 80 then re-write the commandments in the positive as "Thou Shalts."

© Copyright 2001, Veritas Press | 800-922-5082

Worksheet

1. What is the date for the Ten Commandments?

2. What is the Scripture reference for the Ten Commandments?

3. What did God give to Moses on Mt. Sinai?

4. With what were the Ten Commandments written?

5. List the Ten Commandments in order.

1. _____

2. _____

3. _____

4. _____

5. _____

6. _____

7. _____

8. _____

9. _____

10. _____

Project 1—Bible Reading

Read in Exodus 19 about how the Israelites gathered at Mt. Sinai before he gave them the Ten Commandments. Then fill in the words below that complete the sentences. Use the number of blanks to help you find the correct answer.

1. The people consecrated themselves and washed their _____. (Genesis 19:10)

2. Moses was to set _____ around the mountain, and no one was to _____ it. (Genesis 19:12)

3. On the third day a thick _____ was on the mountain. (Genesis 19:16)

4. Mt. Sinai was all in _____, because the Lord descended upon it in _____. The whole mountain _____. (Genesis 19:18) Moses was up on Mt. Sinai for forty days when God was giving him the Ten Commandments. While Israel was camped at Mt. Sinai God gave them laws and guidelines other than the Ten Commandments.

Aaron and the Golden Calf

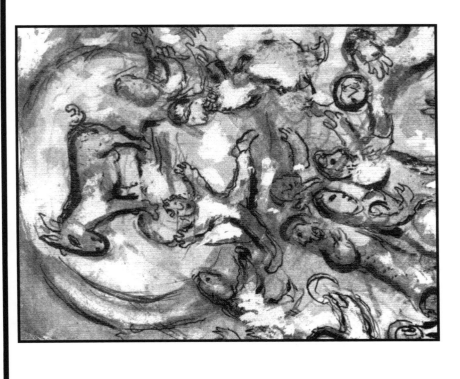

Project 2—Drama

Students can really remember that which they explain or act out. Assign students parts as suggested below. Allow the students to come up with the dialog from their own knowledge of the story. It is suggested that the story be acted out several times. Switch parts each time.

CAST OF CHARACTERS:

Aaron

Moses

Voice of God

Golden Calf

Israelites

 © Copyright 2001, Veritas Press | 800-922-5082

Worksheet

1. What is the date for this card?

2. What is the Scripture reference for this card?

3. What did the Israelites ask Aaron to do?

4. What did God want to do because of the sin of the Israelites?

5. What did Moses do when he came down the mountain and saw the golden calf?

6. What did Moses' actions show?

7. How did Moses act as a mediator between God and the people?

8. How is Moses like Jesus?

Project 1—Bible Reading

Read Exodus 32 and write a paragraph telling what happened when Moses came down the mountain. Be sure to include what happened to the tablets and the golden calf. Also include what was the people's punishment.

Moses Gets
New Tablets

Project 2—Mediators

Color in the illustrations representing the two mediators that have gone between God and man.

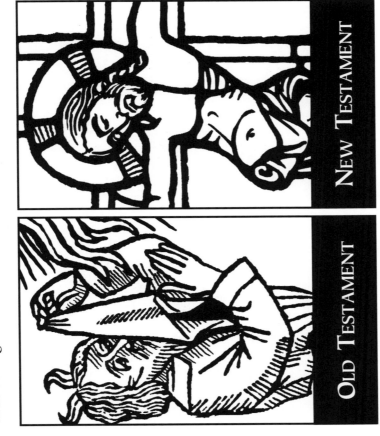

OLD TESTAMENT

NEW TESTAMENT

 © Copyright 2001, Veritas Press | 800-922-5082

Worksheet

1. What is the date of Moses Gets New Tablets?

2. What is the Scripture reference for Moses Gets New Tablets?

3. What did God have Moses make?

4. The Israelites were described as stiff-necked like _____.

5. What did God warn the Israelites not to do?

6. What was to happen to the firstborn animals?

7. How long was Moses on the mountain?

8. What was strange about Moses when he came back down?

9. What did Moses have to wear after he came down the mountain?

Project 1—Bible Reading

Read about Moses receiving new tablets in Exodus 34. Unscramble the words below on the left. Then draw a line to connect the words with the phrases on the right that they correctly complete.

LETBATS	_____ days
ISAIN	observe the _____
FRONTBIRS	new stone _____
BASTBAH	no _____ or water
IFTSF-DENKEC	_____ people
TRYOF	on Mt. _____
BADER	covered with a _____
HINSING	sacrifice the _____
EVIL	a _____ face

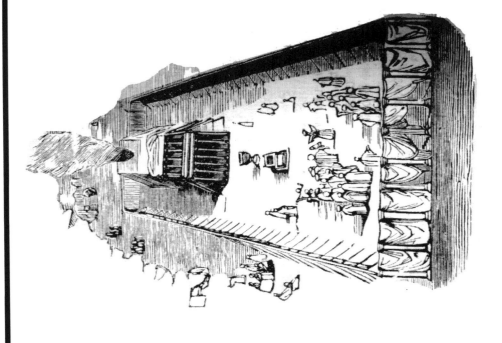

The Tabernacle and the Ark of the Covenant

Project 2

The picture on the right of the Ark is inaccurate. Read the description of what Bezeel had to make in Exodus 25:10–32 and cherubim in Ezekiel 10:14, then draw what the Ark might have looked like on another sheet of paper or in the box provided.

© Copyright 2001, Veritas Press | 800-922-5082

Worksheet

1. What is the date for this card?

2. What is the Scripture reference for this card?

3. Who were two of the main craftsmen that worked on the tabernacle?

4. What did Moses have to do since the people were giving so much money for the building of the tabernacle?

5. Describe the tabernacle.

6. Name three things that were in the tabernacle.

7. Describe the ark of the covenant.

8. What did the High Priest do once a year?

9. The things kept in the ark of the covenant all reminded the people of God's _____.

Project 1—Bible Reading

Read the description of the Tabernacle and Ark in Exodus 36, 37. Inside the four circles below are categories for which you will find examples in the Biblical description of the Ark and the Tabernacle. The circles have spaces for 2, 3, or 4 examples of each category. Fill up the circles with examples from the Biblical description. To get you started, there is an example for each circle in the Example box below.

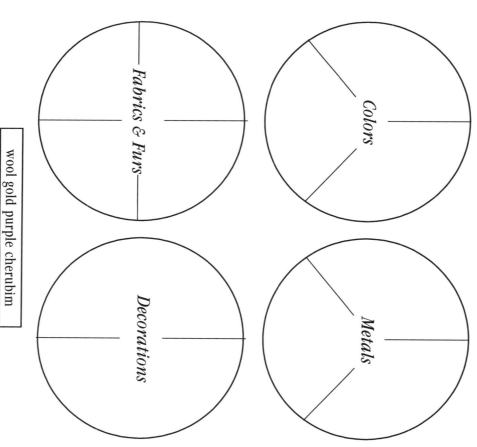

Colors

Metals

Fabrics & Furs

Decorations

wool gold purple cherubim

The Levitical Priesthood Begins

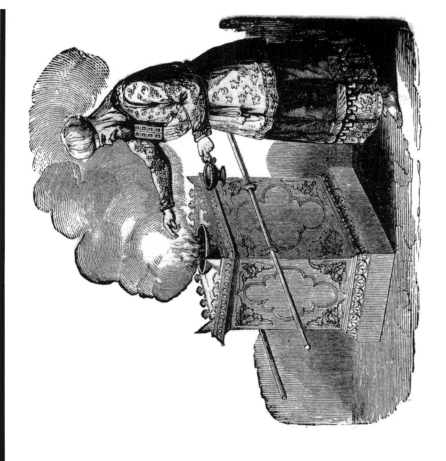

Project 2

Read in Exodus 39 about the clothing of a priest. Then color the picture of the priest.

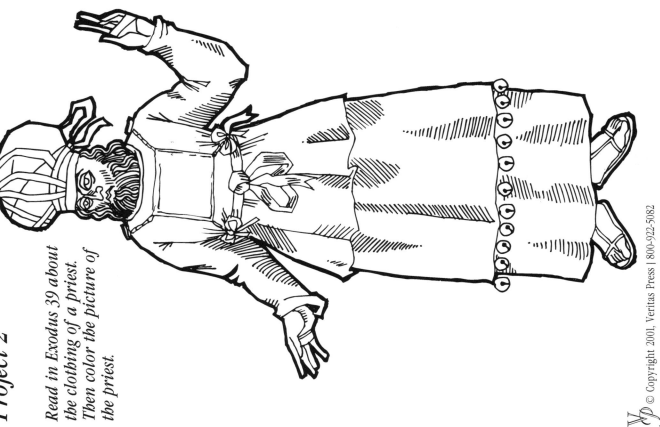

© Copyright 2001, Veritas Press | 800-922-5082

Worksheet

1. What is the date for this card?

2. What is the Scripture reference for this card?

3. Who was given the jobs of carrying the tabernacle and helping the sons of Aaron?

4. Since there were more firstborns than Levites, what did the people have to do?

5. When the Israelites moved into the Promised Land, why weren't the Levites given any land of their own?

6. What is a priest?

7. Who is our perfect High Priest?

Project 1—Bible Reading

Read in Numbers 3 about the beginning of the Levitical priesthood. Complete the word find below, and be sure to know what each word has to do with this event.

```
L E V I S S E R P H A B C D L E
K J I H O F F E R I N G S G A F
L M T N B V C X Z A S D F G M H
L C A M P K C U R T A I N S P J
L P B P O O I U Y T T R E W S W
Q L E V I T E S W E R T Y U T I
I O R P A S D F G H J K L L A Z
Z X N C D V B O B A R K N A N M
I U A Y U U T R U L E W R Q D M
O P C P O I T U S T S O Y T R E
W Q L Q W E R I T A N M N B V C
R S E R V E S E E R W U S Q Z X
T Y Y U I O P L K S J H M G F D
S A Z F I R S T B O R N V B S C
A R O N A A R R O N S A L T E S
T A B E R N A C K L E S L T E R
```

Levites
serve
tabernacle
firstborn
ark

duties
Aaron
camp
offering

curtain
lampstand
altar
outnumber

Project 2—Cartooning

On another sheet of paper draw a comic strip illustrating this story. Your comic strip must contain at least four scenes. Use dialog bubbles to include important things that were said.

The Wilderness Wanderings

© Copyright 2001, Veritas Press | 800-922-5082

Worksheet

Project 1—Bible Reading

Read in Numbers 13, 14 about the scouting mission in to Canaan and the people's response and consequences. In the space provided below list at least five details or facts that were not printed on your card.

1. What is the date for this card?

2. What is the Scripture reference for this card?

3. How trusting were the Israelites during the wilderness wanderings?

4. Fill in the blanks with what God provided when they grumbled for the following things:

   water _____

   food _____

   meat _____

5. How many spies were sent to scout out the land of Canaan?

6. How many spies thought they could defeat the Canaanites?

7. How did God punish the Israelites for not believing that God would help them defeat the Canaanites?

8. How did God lead his people through the wilderness?

9. What happened to all of the adults who had not trusted God to enter the Promised Land?

_____

_____

_____

_____

_____

_____

_____

_____

_____

_____

Balaam and his Donkey

Project 2—Pin the words on the donkey

Play a variation on "Pin the Tail on the Donkey" with words that Balaam's donkey said. Put pictures of Balaam, Balak, and the donkey on a large piece of butcher paper. Make a set of the three quotes for each player. Put a tape doughnut on the back of each quote. Blindfold one player. Read the player a quote and have them try to place it at the mouth of the one that said it. Let them try to correctly place all three quotes. A player wins if he touches each quote with the mouth who said it.

I'LL PAY YOU TO CURSE THE ISRAELITES.

WHY DO YOU STRIKE ME LIKE THIS?

I HAVE BEEN COMMANDED BY GOD TO BLESS AND NOT CURSE ISRAEL.

© Copyright 2001, Veritas Press | 800-922-5082

Worksheet

1. What is the date for this card?
2. What is the Scripture reference for this card?
3. Why did the Moabites fear Israel?
4. Whom did the Moabites hire to curse Israel?
5. Describe Balaam.
6. What did God put in Balaam's path?
7. Why did Balaam's donkey go off the road and then sit down?
8. What miraculous power did God give the donkey?
9. What happened when Balaam tried to curse the Israelites?

Project 1–Bible Reading

Read in Numbers 22-24 about Balaam, Balak, and the donkey. Using your Bible, find who said each quote below. Write their name in the blank. The quotes are listed in the order in which they are found in the story.

1. _____ "Look, a people has come from Egypt. See, they cover the face of the earth, and are settling next to me!"

2. _____ "If the men come to call you, rise and go with them, but only the word which I speak to you—that you shall do."

3. _____ "What have I done to you that you have struck me these three times?"

4. _____ "I have sinned, for I did not know You stood in the way against me. Now therefore, if it displeases You, I will turn back."

5. _____ "What have you done to me? I took you to curse my enemies, and look, you have blessed them bountifully!"

6. _____ "Did I not tell you, saying, 'All that the Lord speaks, that I must do?"

Moses Dies; Joshua Assumes Command

Project 2—Bible Reading

Read Deuteronomy 34. Write a sentence using each of the words below, explaining its use in the story.

CROSS OVER _____

_____

_____

_____

BURIED _____

_____

_____

FACE TO FACE _____

_____

_____

© Copyright 2001, Veritas Press | 800-922-5082

Worksheet

1. What is the date for this card?

2. What is the Scripture reference for this card?

3. Why did God not allow Moses to enter the Promised Land?

4. From what mountain could Moses view the Promised Land?

5. What happened to Moses' body after he died?

6. Who became the new leader of the Israelites after Moses died?

7. What does Joshua's name mean?

8. Why did Moses stand with Joshua before all the people?

Project 1—Obituary

An obituary is a writing used in newspapers to let people know of the death of community members and pay a last tribute to that person. *Write an obituary for Moses on the next page. Include how old he was (check your Bible), describe the event of his death, and briefly tell at least three things he did or stories about him.*

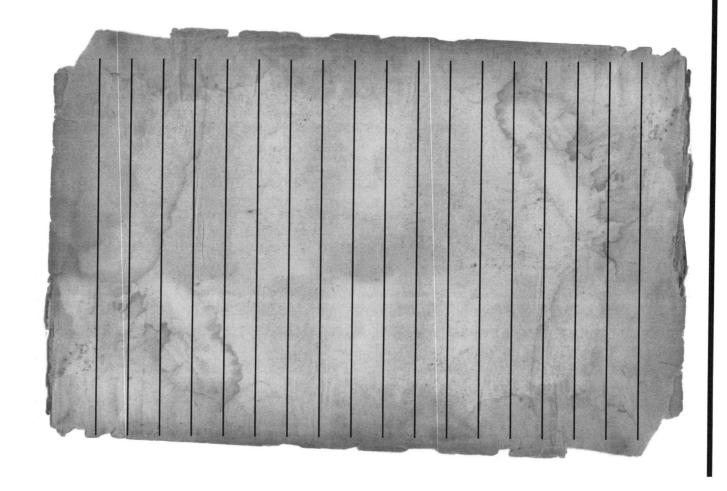

Spies to Canaan

Project 2–Thank You Note

The Hebrew spies sent into Jericho had much for which to be thankful. They particularly were indebted to Rahab. Assume you are one of the two spies that was sent to scout out Jericho. Write a thank-you letter to Rahab on another piece of paper from the perspective of one of the spies. You may be creative when it comes to your name or details about yourself as the Bible gives no description about these men. But you must include at least five points from the story in your letter. Be sure to use the correct format for a friendly letter shown on the right.

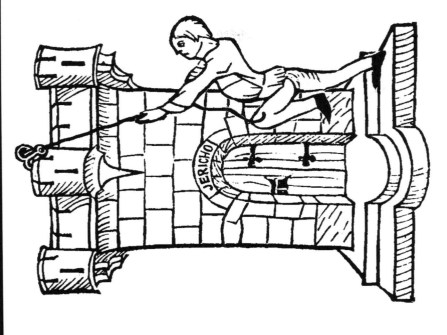

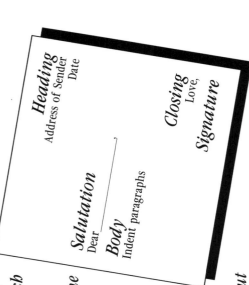

Heading
Address of Sender
Date

Salutation
Dear

Body
Indent paragraphs

Closing
Love,
Signature

© Copyright 2001, Veritas Press | 800-922-5082

Worksheet

1. What is the date for Spies to Canaan?

2. What is the Scripture reference for Spies to Canaan?

3. What city was the first target for the Hebrews in their conquest of the Promised Land?

4. Where did the Israelite spies find lodging and protection?

5. Why did the people of Jericho fear the Israelites and want to capture the Israelite spies?

6. How did the Israelite spies escape from being captured?

7. How was Rahab blessed for her trust in God?

8. Who is Rahab's famous son?

Project 1—Bible Reading

After reading the account of this story in the Bible you will know some specifics that were not included on the card.

Where did Rahab hide the spies?

_____

Which mighty act of God against the Egyptians caused Rahab's people to fear?

_____

_____

_____

What was Rahab to do in order to be spared?

_____

_____

_____

The Battle of Jericho

Project 2

Write a newspaper article from the perspective of a citizen in Jericho. Your article in the Jericho Journal should describe what has been happening outside of your city.

Jericho Journal

© Copyright 2001, Veritas Press | 800-922-5082

Worksheet

1. What is the date for the Battle of Jericho?

2. What is the Scripture reference for the Battle of Jericho?

3. What did the commander of the army of heaven show Joshua?

4. What did the fighting men do for six days?

5. What did the fighting men do on the seventh day?

6. What happened to the walls of Jericho?

7. Who was spared from among the people of Jericho?

8. How did the Israelites know which household was to be spared?

Project 1—Bible Reading

Read about the Battle of Jericho in Joshua 5:13–6:27. Then put the following events in order:

___ The Israelites and the ark marched around Jericho seven times

___ The people shouted

___ The Israelites marched around the city of Jericho once and returned to camp

___ The Israelite army rushed into the city and destroyed everything and everyone except Rahab

___ The Israelite army marched in silence once around the city for the next five days

___ The priests blew their trumpets

___ The commander of the army of the Lord met with Joshua

___ Jericho was burned

___ The walls of Jericho fell down

Israel Given the Promised Land

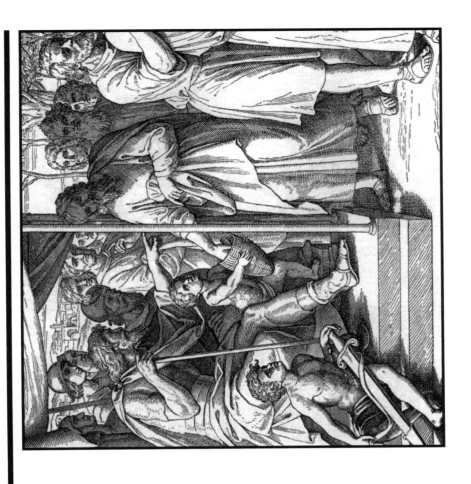

Project 2—Military Medals

Supplies
Ribbon (at least 1" wide)
construction paper
metallic finished paper
metallic colored spray paint
beads, sequins
safety pins

Directions
Medals can be made by taking a 5" long strip of ribbon and folding it in half. Students design the medallion part by using a variety of supplies provided by you (some are suggested here). Glue the medallion part to the two ends of ribbon. Concealing the head of the pin in between the folded ribbon, run the point through the back half of the ribbon.

© Copyright 2001, Veritas Press | 800-922-5082

Worksheet

1. What is the date for this card?

2. What is the Scripture reference for this card?

3. Why were the Israelites able to conquer the Canaanites?

4. How were the Israelites disobedient to God's command?

5. What two things did the Israelites allow the Canaanites to do?

6. How did the Canaanites cause problems for many years after the conquest?

7. Which tribe was the most faithful during the conquest?

Project 1—Bible Reading

Read Joshua 21:43–45 and Judges 1:8–36. Then complete the crossword puzzle below.

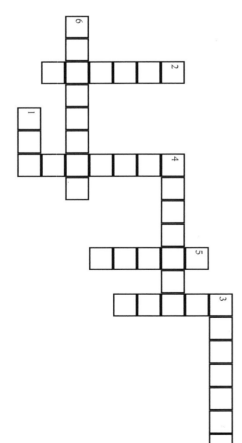

ACROSS
1. _____ gave Israel the Promised Land.
3. God told Israel to _____ all of the Canaanites.
4. Some Israelites allowed their enemies to pay them
6. Judah was not successful in the lowland because the people there used _____. (Judges 1:19)

DOWN
2. The land of _____ was the Promised Land.
3. Many of the Canaanites were allowed to _____ in the land.
4. The Israelites were _____ to follow the false gods of the Canaanites.
5. _____ was the only tribe that was obedient to God's